Teenagers
Preparing for the Real World

Chad Foster

dedication

To my mother Malise, who taught me nothing about
making a living, but everything about living.

To my father David, who raised me like a son,
but treated me like a friend.

To my sister Elise, who believed in this project
even before I did.

To my brother Patch, who will always hold a
special place in my heart.

Teenagers
Preparing for the Real World

Chad Foster

Autographed Copies

To order personally autographed copies of
Teenagers—Preparing for the Real World
visit our website at www.chadfoster.com

Spanish Version

To order the Spanish version of
Teenagers—Preparing for the Real World
call (770) 761-8794.

Contents

author's note

As long as I can remember, traveling and meeting people have been two of my favorite pastimes. I believe there is nothing more interesting than new faces and new places.

Recently, I traveled across the United States and spoke to hundreds of students from all walks of life. I asked them what they wanted to do when they finished school, and almost all said the same thing: "I don't know. I want to be successful, but I don't know where to start."

These were some of the brightest young people I had ever met. While their intelligence impressed me, their confusion surprised me. I wondered how so many young people could be so unclear about preparing for their future.

It's obvious that schools are educating these students. But no one seems to be preparing them for the real world — which is where they will all soon be.

Today, every time you turn around, someone is telling you what not to do: don't do drugs, don't smoke, don't drink, don't sleep till noon, etc. I have a feeling that you've heard enough about what you *can't* do. Maybe the time has come to tell you what you can do if you want to succeed.

Now is the time to begin to understand the value of people skills, networking skills, early career preparation, integrity, communication skills, dreams, and community service. All of these are critical for anyone who wants to succeed, and I believe most teenagers want to succeed.

This book is about the skills of success. It was written for those who want to succeed. What you do now will make a difference.

You are on a journey. It's the same journey that I used to be on. In order for you to succeed on your journey, you will need two things — a good education and good preparation.

Schools were built to educate you. This book was written to prepare you to succeed.

W hen I was a kid — not a teenager, but a kid — I dreamed of growing up and being really rich. I was always making a list of the things I wanted to buy. As I got older, I started buying some of those things that I thought I had to have. Unfortunately, I was always buying stuff that I really couldn't afford, like the Rolex watch I bought when I was 18. I spent every dime I had saved for five years on a watch! My father, Mr. Conservative, went crazy. His watch was a Timex, a $14.99 Wal-Mart special. The minute he saw my Rolex, he took off his Timex, dropped it on the kitchen floor, and threatened to smash it into a million pieces with one stomp of his foot. Never a man short on words, he added commentary to this one-man drama with, "Do you realize I could smash 100 watches like mine before I spent the kind of money you just wasted?"

As usual, most of what he said went in one ear and out the other. I wish I had a dollar for every word of his advice that I didn't listen to when I was younger. I would have been a millionaire at 17. Maybe then I could have bought him his own Rolex.

As time went on, I finally figured out why I was buying so many things. I thought they made me look successful. I didn't need them,

> **"Now Mama said,** 'There's only so much money a man really needs, and the rest is just for showing off.'"
>
> Forrest Gump
> in the movie FORREST GUMP

I just wanted them. It took me 15 years to understand the difference between need and want, and to finally understand the real meaning of success.

When I was a teenager, I thought if I went to school, made good grades, and got a degree, I would get a great job, make lots of money, and be very successful. I wasn't sure what a great job was, what a lot of money was, or even what the real meaning of success was. But it all sounded pretty good to me, and I just assumed I would figure it out when I got older. It took me 15 years to figure it out. Please don't let that happen to you.

How are you supposed to figure all of this out? When should you start thinking about your future? Are some people born lucky, or do they get lucky as time goes on? Why do some people hit home runs while others strike out?

Who cares? Nobody, except those of us who want to succeed.

So maybe you're someone who wants to succeed. What is success? What is a lot of money? What is a great job? And most importantly, what do you have to do to succeed?

That's enough questions to make you dizzy. This book will try to answer those questions.

I was lucky enough to take a break from work when I was 33. Since then, I have traveled the world and learned a lot about life. Along the way, I've met some incredible people. Thanks to them, I finally understand what success really means.

I was in California for a day with Elton John; in New York with Laurie Stephenson, star of Broadway's *Phantom of the Opera;* in Birmingham, Alabama, for a little baseball with Michael Jordan; and at the White House for a workout with Arnold Schwarzenegger.

I also spent time with lots of successful people who aren't famous — successful people from all walks of life. From everyone I met, both famous and not so famous, I learned that success is a journey, not a destination. They also convinced me that where you start on your journey to success has nothing to do with where you finish. On the other hand, *when* you start on your journey has a lot to do with where you finish.

Now I understand that where you grow up, the house you live in, the jobs your parents have, and the car your parents drive have nothing to do with your ability to succeed.

I also learned from the successful people I met that there are two kinds of success — professional and personal. I learned that professional success without personal success is not worth much. Professional success is good. Personal success is better. And fortunately, you can have both.

Professional success means different things to different people — maybe it's a big house or an expensive car — but personal success should be the same for everyone. Personal success is about having good friends, good family, and liking your job. It's also about making a contribution to the community you live in.

This book was written to prepare you to succeed. I hope that when you achieve that goal, your definition of success will be similar to mine.

When I was 27, I had an idea. I developed a product that makes playgrounds safer for kids. You probably drive by that product every day. Next time you're at McDonald's, look into the playground and watch the kid fall from the top of the slide. When you see him crash to the ground, you might expect his brains to spill out, but they won't. The kid's okay because he fell on the rubber surface that I developed. It's soft, it's safe, and it's made of recycled tires that are ground up and mixed with a polyurethane binder. In fact, it's the most popular playground surface in the United States. It was just a simple idea. Maybe it wasn't so simple. McDonald's paid millions of dollars to have the surface installed at 3,000 of their playgrounds, and then Disney World bought it, too. The product was a huge success. But hey, we're talking no brain-spills here — and millions, for no brain-spills, is a bargain.

Since the surface is made from recycled rubber, a great use has been found for recycled tires. The product I developed keeps tires out of land-fills, where they would otherwise be buried for a zillion years. In fact, over 10 million pounds of recycled tire rubber has found its way into playgrounds around the world.

How did I know how to do what I did? You might say I took one of the roads less traveled.

I'm sure a degree in chemistry would have come in handy as I invented a product that combined methylene dephenyl isocyanate and styrene butadiene rubber. And I'm sure a marketing degree would have been helpful as I marketed our product to the world's largest playground clients. Unfortunately, my degree is not in chemistry or marketing. I have no degree. I was a college dropout.

Hang on. Don't get excited. This book is *not* about quitting school. Quitting school will not help anyone become successful. In fact, it will make success much tougher to attain. If you quit school, your chances of succeeding are probably 1 out of 100. Those are tough odds. If you don't think so, ask one of your friends to pick a number between one and 100. Then try to guess the number that she picked. Your chances of guessing correctly are 1 out of 100. Try it a few times. See how you do.

Some people who quit school do become successful. But I can tell you from experience that quitting school makes it tougher, not easier.

I was forced to choose an alternate road in preparing for my professional future. It was the highway of trial and error and it was paved with the relationships and skills that I developed as a teenager. I could not have survived without them. The more education you get, the better off you will be.

When my parents were teenagers, a high school degree was a must if you wanted to get a good job and succeed. When my generation came along, we were told that a college degree was necessary for success. But what about your generation? What will it take for you to succeed? Is a degree all you need? A lot has changed over the past few years. Changes in the corporate culture (layoffs, mergers, downsizing, etc.) have created many new challenges for future employees. You and your classmates are those future employees.

Now students everywhere are confused and concerned because they don't know what to expect when they get out of school. They are smart and they are educated, but they are not fully prepared to enter the real world. This is sad. And it's not fair to you. We owe you a good map so you can succeed on your journey.

I happen to think that students today are considerably brighter than in years past. You are probably too bright to be taught with the same old methods of the past. Teaching is the art of stimulating the student, and it is painfully obvious that we are having a difficult time stimulating your generation. Yours is not a generation that is easily stimulated. Thank goodness. Maybe you will motivate us to fix a system that needs improvement. Hopefully, we will recognize your needs for more preparation to go along with your formal education.

Everybody is busy trying to educate you. This is good. But not enough time is being spent preparing you for the real world. This is bad. The purpose of this book is not to diminish the importance of a formal education. Quitting school is not the answer. The answer is a combination of two things — the knowledge that you will gain in school and the skills of success that you will learn outside of school.

This book is all about the skills that you might not learn in school.

The

Skills

of

Success

a kid at camp

Most journeys have a start, a finish, and a turning point somewhere in between. The turning point in my journey came earlier than I expected. I was only 13 years old, but that's when it happened, and that's really what this book is about. I want you to see that there are many things you can do while you're young that will make your road to success much shorter and much smoother.

When I was 13, my parents informed me that they had signed me up for eight weeks of camp in North Carolina. It seems like all kids go to some sort of summer camp when they become teenagers. My older sister had been for three summers already, and loved it. Most young people love camp. Camp is supposed to be fun.

I hated camp.

I was miserable from the day I arrived. The food stunk, my counselor was a loser, and my new girlfriend was back home in Louisiana. I called my parents collect every night, begging them to let me come home. Finally, my parents refused to accept one of those calls. They thought quitting camp was a bad idea. I was thinking child abuse. They were thinking it was time for me to grow up.

There I was, on a mountain in North Carolina, with 300 strangers. I couldn't believe I was going to waste my last summer before high school in the middle of nowhere, with a bunch of kids I didn't even know.

Let me be perfectly clear: I hated camp.

My cabin sat high on a hill, next to the tennis courts. Since I didn't even play tennis, that was no big deal to me. Of greater concern was the fact that my cabin location also forced me to walk all the way down the hill to the outhouse in the middle of the night. Most guys just went behind the cabin and watered the plants, but not me. I preferred to walk down the hill, sometimes twice a night. That gave me one more thing to gripe about on my nightly call home to the parents.

My counselor's name was Norville Rose. I don't think we ever got along very well. Who would name their kid Norville, anyway? I thought he was a horrible counselor, and I'm sure I made his life miserable that summer. But listen to this.

Fast-forward 10 years. I was in Denver, Colorado, on business. I checked into my hotel and flipped on the TV to catch the evening news. A handsome, talented anchorman was delivering that day's top story. As he finished, I heard a voice-over announce, "That's the Nightly News with Norville Rose."

I freaked. I knew it couldn't be *the* Norville Rose, but then again, how could two sets of parents both come up with a name like that? The next morning I called my friend Frank, who was running my former camp in North Carolina. I asked him if he knew what my old counselor was up to these days. He said, "Sure, he's the top news anchor in Denver, Colorado. I always knew he'd be a big success. Don't you remember? He was one of our finest counselors."

"Right," I said. "Good old Norville. What a great guy." So much for my opinion.

I remember camp and my battles with Norville like it was yesterday. I couldn't stand rest hour. Naps were for old people. There were too many rules. I was 13, not 6. Why was he always telling me to make my bed? It was *my* bed, wasn't it? I don't remember telling him what to do with *his* bed. Every time I had taken all I could from Norville, and vice versa, I would head out the front door of my cabin and sit in the only place I could — on the tennis courts. After several days of hanging out on the courts, one of the tennis counselors walked over to me and asked if I'd like to join his class. He introduced himself as Murphy Sweeney. I knew we would get along the minute I heard his name. Murphy Sweeney. Now, that's a great name! It

wasn't until five years later that I would find out that Murphy Sweeney wasn't his real name after all. But even his real name wasn't as bad as Norville Rose.

Murphy taught me a lot about life, but most importantly, he taught me how to play tennis.

Like most boys, I grew up playing football, baseball, and basketball. These sports taught me a lot about competition and the importance of teamwork. Whether it's a soccer team, a debate team, or a 40-member band, working together and sharing responsibilities are important for success. Sometimes you win, sometimes you lose. That's the way it is in the real world, too.

Winning isn't everything, but it's a whole lot better than losing. But even losing serves a purpose. When you lose — in sports or in business — you learn. And when you learn, you improve. And guess what? When you improve, you win more.

Recently, I heard Michael Jordan say something that I thought was pretty interesting. In one of his new television commercials Michael says, "I have missed 9,000 shots during my career. My teams have lost 300 games. And 26 times that my teammates gave me the ball in the final seconds of the game to take the game-winning shot, I missed the shot and we lost the game. I have failed over and over and over again." But then Michael says, "The only reason I can succeed is because I understand how to deal with failure." Failure is part of every journey.

Even in tennis, the sport I played as a kid — where credit for winning and blame for losing goes to an individual instead of a team — winning is still winning and losing is still learning.

I was hooked on tennis from the start. I was on the courts every day, morning till night. As soon as I realized that I had been blessed with this ability, a big question hit me right in the face. What would I do with this newly discovered talent? Use it? Abuse it? Waste it? Little did I know what a huge role tennis would play in my future.

I never returned to camp as a kid. And I never played baseball, basketball, or football again either. Under the guidance of Murphy Sweeney, I developed my God-given talent, a talent that became the basis for much of my success, or good luck, depending on how you look at it.

As I look back with 20/20 hindsight (which is easy to do many years later), I'm sure that camp was one of my most valuable experiences. I learned more about life in eight weeks on a mountain than some people learn in a lifetime. I learned the importance of meeting new people and I learned that things don't always go your way. These might seem like simple lessons, but they are two of the most important lessons a person can learn.

While camp taught me the importance of meeting new people, tennis made it possible for me to meet those people. I spent the next summer traveling from city to city on the junior tennis circuit. I was lucky enough to become one of America's top-ranked players and travel across the United States and Europe to compete against some of the world's best. As I traveled, I met hundreds of new people that I would stay in touch with for years to come. Over the years, these people became my friends, my clients, and my business associates. They became my future.

It seems kind of funny now. There I was, thinking camp was a big waste of time. But in fact, camp was where I learned some of my most valuable skills. Thank goodness my parents didn't let me quit. Just think: no camp, no tennis. And maybe no future.

the music man

Tennis had become my passion. At the time, I had no idea what a passion was. Now I do, and I understand its importance. Life without a passion is dull, boring, and without much purpose.

What is a passion?

According to Webster — a man of many words — a passion is defined as "something that one greatly likes or desires."

A passion is an intense affection that you develop for something you are introduced to. That's *something*, not *someone*. Your passion might be music or reading or travel. It might be the homeless, the environment, or AIDS education. Your passion might change as you get older. In fact, it probably will.

In case you're wondering what your passion might be, think of something you do that makes you forget everything else. Is there something you do that turns a bad day into a good one? What is the first thing you want to do if you have some free time? Maybe there's something you do that helps you forget your problems for a while. As long as it's legal, it just might be your passion.

> **"The most important things in life aren't things."**
>
> Anonymous

Speaking of passion, I'll never forget the day I met Elton John. My brother was a friend of Elton's, and he invited me out to Elton's home in California. I was out west that week anyway, so the invitation was most timely. Come to think of it, though, it really wouldn't have made any difference where I was that week. I was a huge Elton John fan and happened to be reading a book about his life. In my opinion, Elton is a legend, and I wouldn't have dreamed of passing up an opportunity to meet him personally.

I arrived at Elton's home at noon to find him right in the middle of lunch. As always for Elton, lunch consisted of only healthy items — fresh fish, fresh fruit, and fresh juices. Elton doesn't drink, smoke, or do drugs — any more. As the day went on, I listened to Elton tell stories about the drugs and alcohol that almost ruined his career and, more tragically, almost killed him. I believe he speaks openly about his past so that we can learn from his experiences. This makes more sense than living his experiences and, if we survive, learning from them.

The book I was reading about Elton referred often to a childhood of turmoil, low self-esteem, and strained relations between Elton and his biological father. It told a story of very difficult teenage years. Elton's story made me understand how important it is to have someone to talk to when you think your life is spinning out of control or when you're totally depressed or even when you're just having a rotten day. Who do you talk to when you don't feel so great?

I sat on the couch in Elton's living room as he played a few songs on the piano. As he played, I wondered how Elton made it through those difficult times. After talking to him, the answer was obvious. It was music that made the bad days bearable. Music is his passion.

Elton John was anything but an instant success. In spite of training at the Royal Academy of Music in England, he struggled for years as a young musician. Since fortune and fame had not yet arrived, something else had to inspire him. It was his love for music — his passion that kept him going.

Never underestimate the power of your passion.

I learned a lot from Elton that day. He rented a bus — fully equipped with a television, sofas, and a refrigerator — to take us to Magic Mountain theme park for the day. It was a real pleasure to spend the day with a musical legend like Elton. As we made our way through Magic Mountain, security surrounding us, I was amazed by the crowds swarming around Elton. They were fighting their way through the mob just for a glance at Elton John, the superstar, screaming hysterically in the hope that their voices might get his attention. It struck me as odd that these people were so fanatic about a man they had never met, much less spoken with. They were obviously in awe of Elton's musical talents and his public persona. I wanted to tell them what I had learned about the private Elton — beyond the piano, the stage, and the costumes. I wished I could tell them about this man who overcame depression, drug addiction, and parental problems at home. I'd tell them about a man who was genuinely concerned about so many other people, and cared so little about fame and wealth. Elton became, and continues to be, a true friend of my family.

From Elton, I learned a lot about the difference between personal success and professional success. I'm glad I had a chance to meet him and to understand how his passion carried him through the tough times and down the road to success.

By the way, what is *your* passion?

the "meet" of the matter

Y ou've probably heard this one: "It's not what you know, it's who you know." I disagree. I believe that what you know and who you know are equally important.

I also believe that what you know about who you know is extremely important.

In addition to what you're learning in school, there are certain skills that will greatly improve your chances of succeeding in the real world. These skills are communication skills, networking skills, and people skills.

All successful business people can point to one item that is the key to their success. It's never a $20,000 phone system, a $5,000 computer, or a $400 desk. It's almost always a $9.95 Rolodex. Rolodex is just a fancy name for an address book. The names, addresses, and phone numbers found in a Rolodex represent contacts that are made by its owner. These contacts are made and developed over many years. They are a definite key to success. I wouldn't sell my list of contacts and the

> "A wise man knows everything. A smart man knows everyone. A successful man knows both."
>
> Ancient Chinese Proverb

relationships that go with them for a million dollars. In the real world, the person with the most contacts has a huge advantage.

Who are these contacts?

They are the acquaintances you make as you travel through life. They are your classmates, your teammates, your parents' friends, and your friends' parents. They are the people you meet at work, at church, at the mall, etc.

In the future, these contacts will become your clients, your customers, your colleagues, your employers, and your solutions to problems. They will be your advisors, your mentors, and your friends. You will learn from them and lean on them. These are contacts. They are not connections. They are not people that you meet, use, and then throw away. These are contacts and your relationship with them is a two-way street. Over the years, you will help them and they will help you.

Quite simply, these contacts are your future.

When should you begin making these contacts? Today. Tomorrow is too late. Don't waste today. There will always be another tomorrow to experience new things. But once today has become yesterday, you can't get it back. Those 24 hours are gone for good. Yesterday is only as good as how it was used when it was today.

One of society's greatest myths is the belief that contacts are only made between adults. The average person believes this to be true. The average person is wrong, and this book is not about being average.

When I was 19, I left school for the third time. My grades were good, but I was bored. Sound familiar? I was scared to death to tell my parents that I had left school again. The first couple of times I quit weren't so tough, because I always knew I'd go back. But when I left for the third time, I knew I was done. I put off telling my parents for several weeks. By the time I finally got the nerve to break the news, they had already figured it out. My dad took me to breakfast that Saturday morning, which was a tradition whenever I was home for the weekend. After breakfast, he pulled into the parking lot at his office and parked his little green Toyota as far from the entrance as possible. I had a feeling we weren't going into the office for coffee and donuts.

Radio off. Ignition off. Windows down. When the windows went down, I knew I was in for the long haul. This was his favorite place to give a lecture, so I just sat back and prepared to take my medicine. I will spare you the agony of that next 60 minutes and just share a few of his thoughts.

He reminded me that my grandfather had been an attorney. He didn't need to remind me that he himself was also an attorney. Nor did he need to remind me that I was his oldest son, had been blessed with a good mind, and had a real future in the legal profession. No, he really didn't need to refresh my memory on any of these issues, but he did.

His final remarks were, "You don't know what you're going to do. You don't know where you're going to do it. And now, you won't even have a college education. What if things don't work out for you? What will you fall back on?"

"Fall back." Those two words stuck in my mind like a bad dream. I wondered if he thought I was doomed to fail at whatever I did next. I knew my father was disappointed. But as I would learn later in life, disappointment is something we all have to deal with occasionally.

At my house, when you were out of school you were out of the house. It's not like my parents threw my stuff out into the street, but they did give me a "departure" date. Hello real world. Even worse, I was officially off the parental payroll. Sounded brutal to me at the time, but nothing could have been better for my future.

Since I had no money, no job, and no plan, I did the most practical thing I could think of. I went on a road trip to Florida. I've never believed that worrying could solve a single problem. On the other hand, I've always believed that thinking can solve almost anything. What better place to think than the beaches of Florida?

As I stretched out by the pool at the Ramada Resort on Fort Walton Beach, I looked up at the oceanside hotel rooms and tried to imagine what they were like. I could only imagine, since I had actually spent my last few dollars to stay at a fleabag motel across the street. Okay, so I snuck into the Ramada Resort that day. Give me a break. I had some heavy thinking to do, and I didn't believe a fleabag motel was a very good place to think.

Before I had time to start my heavy thinking, I noticed a guy walking toward my chair. I just knew he was with hotel security and that he was coming over to kick me off the property. I made the transition from thinking to worrying in about four seconds.

To my great surprise, he called me by my name. Now I felt like a real criminal. Not only was he going to kick me out, but he knew who I was. How embarrassing! The sun was in my eyes, so I couldn't see the guy's face. I was expecting handcuffs but got a handshake instead. His name was David Brantley. He was from Louisiana and had just started a company that specialized in the construction of tennis courts. His company was young but growing. He explained that his background was in construction, but he needed some help. He needed a link to the tennis community. David Brantley had the knowledge, but he needed contacts. Fortunately, I had made lots of those.

I was only 19, but I had spent the past six years crisscrossing the country playing tennis. As I traveled, I met hundreds of people from all walks of life. I had filled my address book with the names, addresses, and phone numbers of everyone I met, both young and old. This was one piece of advice that I took from my parents.

I got excited as David and I talked about the company he had started. I couldn't stop thinking about that Saturday morning in the parking lot with my dad. I couldn't wait to call him. It had taken me a while to figure it out, but now I had an answer to his question. I would "fall back" on the contacts I had spent so many years making and developing.

I did fall back on those contacts, and I did work with David Brantley — for 13 great years. We built a multimillion-dollar company that installed tennis courts, running tracks, and yes, even playground surfaces. Throughout my career, I always looked to my contacts for their advice, support, and help. I could not have succeeded without them.

Isn't it amazing that David Brantley and I were in the same city, at the same pool, on the same day? Not really. I don't believe in coincidences.

But he knew my name when he saw me at the pool. How do you explain that? That's easy. I met David Brantley in Dallas, Texas, when I was 15. We met through a mutual friend.

> "I have never let my schooling interfere with my education."
>
> Mark Twain

Who would have thought we would meet again, five years later? Who would have thought we would work together for 13 years? Who would have thought we would build a multimillion-dollar company together?

If you had told me then that I could meet someone when I was 15 with whom I would later build a multimillion-dollar company, I would have laughed in your face. If you told me that same story today, we could laugh together — all the way to the bank.

What happened to me happens to lots of people. And yes, it could easily happen to you. You just never know.

The formula is pretty simple. Success = knowledge + skills + people. The more people you meet, the better your chances of succeeding will be, regardless of which career you ultimately choose.

Here's a great example. What if I come to your school and take you and 99 of your closest friends to the mall. When we get to the mall I will buy every one of you a brand new pair of tennis shoes. Not a bad deal so far, right?

When we arrive at the mall we see a store at the east end that sells every style of tennis shoes you have ever heard of. We also see a store at the west end of the mall that sells every style of tennis shoes available. The prices at both stores are identical. So, the same shoes are available at both stores, and the prices are the same at both stores. The only difference between these two stores is that you and your 99 friends have another really good friend who works, on commission, at the east mall store. Now when we get to the mall, where do you think you will buy your shoes?

Of course, you will buy them from the east mall store where your friend works. Not because the east mall store has a better selection of shoes, and not because the east mall store has better prices. The only reason all 100 of you are going to buy your shoes from the east mall store is because your good friend works there.

This is exactly how it works in the business world, too. People do business with people they know, with people they like, and with their friends. Strangers come last on the list. This is why it's so important for young people to meet as many people as they can. And to stay in touch with everyone they meet. People make people successful.

Some of you may not be comfortable with the idea of meeting new people. Don't let this concern you. Making contacts is a skill that you develop over time. "Develop" is the key word here. Like any skill, this one takes practice to improve. It's not a game. You can't win or lose and no one is keeping score. The secret to making contacts at an early age is simple. You must make an effort to meet new people every day. You can meet these people everywhere: at school, church, camp, the mall, the park, at home, at concerts, on planes, at restaurants, etc. The list goes on and on. Meet all kinds of people: old, young, rich, poor, black, white, gay, straight. The more you meet, the more you grow. The more diversity in the contacts you make, the more you will learn, and the more valuable your contacts will be.

Don't be afraid to talk to people you don't know, especially those who are older than you. I know you probably grew up just like I did, with everyone telling you not to talk to strangers. That was bad advice. They should have told us not to talk to *strange* strangers. There are a lot of people you don't know yet that you need to talk to. These are the people who can help you achieve your dreams and reach your goals. Remember, nobody succeeds in business on their own. Nobody succeeds without help. Now is the time to start talking to strangers. Stop and think about it. Everyone you know today was a stranger before you met them, right?

Never miss a chance to meet a friend of a friend. This is an easy, comfortable contact to make. And who knows? That friend of your friend might have a cousin, who has a brother, who has an aunt, who owns a company that might hire you someday. That, I promise you, is how it works in the real world.

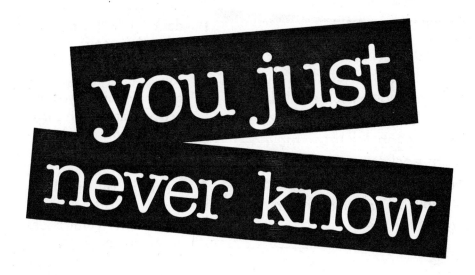

you just never know

Hopefully at this point, the message is clear. Contacts should be made at an early age between young people and older people, between young people and young people, between black people and white people, etc. There is much to be learned from everyone you meet.

Shakespeare once asked, "What's in a name?" The answer I suggest is "nothing," unless, of course, an address and phone number are included and entered into your address book. By the way, if you don't have an address book, get one. If you do have one, fill it. If yours is full, get another one.

When I quit working, I realized I had to tell all of my contacts that I was leaving. As I began to sort through my business cards, Rolodex, and personal address books, I was amazed to learn that I would have to notify almost 2,000 people. For a minute, I thought it might be easier to just keep on working. Two thousand seemed like a lot to me, but I'm sure someone like the president of MTV has a list of 10,000 contacts or more. That's probably why he's the president of MTV.

Meeting people is easy, particularly if you've had some practice. It usually takes very little to strike up a conversation with someone you

> **"In 1962, a kid by the name of Phil Knight accidentally blew his nose with a sock during a job interview. He didn't get the job. He later moved from socks to shoes and today, Mr. Snotty Sock runs a 5 billion dollar company called NIKE."**

don't know. I can assure you that any time a younger person initiates a conversation with someone older, that younger person earns immediate respect, and a relationship is born. Relationships, not connections, are what you are looking for. Relationships are long-term; connections are often short-term.

When you strike up a conversation with someone new, remember to refer to that person by name as often as possible. This will make the communication more personal and will help you remember the person's name later on. As the conversation comes to a close, ask your new acquaintance for his or her address and phone number at work. Ask for a business card if your new contact is in business. Turn the card over and make a note of where and when you met this person as well as anything else you think you should remember about the person. Tell your new acquaintance that you enjoyed your time together and that you would like to stay in touch. Whatever you do, please forget two things during this whole ordeal: your age and your new acquaintance's age. Age doesn't matter.

Here's a great example. I went out for dinner in Atlanta recently. While waiting for a table, I sat next to a Japanese man who appeared to be in his early fifties. He was in formal business attire. I was all dressed up in NIKE sweats and running shoes. I immediately knew three things: first, he was obviously much older than I; second, he was definitely more dressed up than I; and third, it was possible that he didn't even speak English.

I didn't care. I went ahead and did what I always do. I looked over at him and asked a question: "Have you eaten here before?" I tried English, since I didn't know one word of Japanese. Remember, I had no idea who this guy was. He could have been in the Mafia, for all I knew. He wasn't. His name is Eddy Koike and he was the president of the Suntory Corporation. Suntory is a Japanese conglomerate with a half-billion dollars in annual sales. That's billion with a "b." He answered my question — in English, thank goodness. He said, "Yes, the food here is very good."

I guess he did like the food. His company owned the restaurant. And that's not all. Mr. Koike's company owned several businesses in the U.S., so I had tons of questions to ask him. He seemed pleased that someone my age was so interested in his business. I bet I asked him 20 questions. Before we left the restaurant, I exchanged addresses with Mr. Koike. I shook his hand and told him that I looked forward to seeing him in Birmingham the following week. Did I forget to mention that Mr. Koike's company also owned a minor league baseball team in Birmingham, Alabama? And did I mention that Michael Jordan played for his team? I guess I also forgot to tell you that Mr. Koike invited me to join him at the next home game. We watched that game from the front row, behind home plate, all because I started a conversation with a stranger.

Some contacts you make will have an immediate impact on your life, like Mr. Koike did on mine. Others may impact your life within months. It is possible, however, that some new contacts will not affect your life until several years later.

With this in mind, consider the importance of communication — of staying in touch with your newly made contacts. You meet them, you exchange addresses and phone numbers, and then you go your separate ways. You might go to different cities, different states, or even different countries.

TIME OUT. STOP READING. TURN OFF THE MUSIC. TURN OFF THE TELEVISION. TELL EVERYONE TO LEAVE THE ROOM. THIS NEXT PARA-GRAPH IS CRITICAL TO SUCCESS. YOU MIGHT WANT TO READ IT TWICE.

At this point, you have only made your contact. Now you must develop the relationship. You will do this through communication of all sorts. You will stay in touch by mail, by phone, and in person; at Christmas, on birthdays, and on special occasions; in good times and in bad times. Most importantly, you will send thank-you notes to your new contacts for their advice, their hospitality, their generosity, and their efforts on your behalf. Every time you communicate with your new acquaintances, they learn more about you, and you learn more about them. The more you know about each other, the stronger your relationship will be. You should stay in touch with all of your contacts, whether they have affected your life yet or not.

Communication is the key that unlocks the door to success for young people like you.

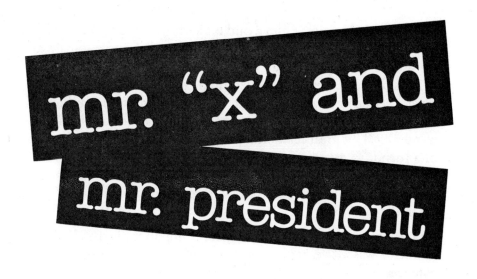

mr. "x" and mr. president

When I was 18, I took my first sabbatical from college. Sabbatical is a politically correct term that parents use when they are too embarrassed to tell their friends that their son quit school. I packed my car in Tallahassee, Florida, and headed for California to take my chances on the professional tennis tour. My first stop was Austin, Texas, where I planned to spend a few days practicing before heading west. When I arrived at my hotel in Austin, I ran into a friend from my hometown in Louisiana. Coincidence? I'm not so sure.

My friend was in Austin on vacation with some of his friends who I did not know. One of the friends was a man in his late forties. Remember, I was just 18 years old at the time.

I hit it off right away with this man. Let's just call him Mr. "X" for now. I played tennis with Mr. X a few times, and joined him and my hometown friend for dinner. When I left Austin a couple of days later, I exchanged addresses with Mr. X and promised to stay in touch with him. Our paths wouldn't cross again until several years later.

During that time, I made every effort to stay in touch with Mr. X. We exchanged letters periodically. I mailed him postcards from my travels and I always sent him a card on his birthday, not because I had to, but because I wanted to. I called him for advice occasionally, and we always corresponded at Christmas. Our brief acquaintance in Texas slowly evolved into a friendship that is almost 20 years old. Over a period of several years, Mr. X referred almost one million dollars worth of business to me, not because he had to, but because he wanted to. This great relationship was possible because I met a friend of a friend, in Austin, Texas, when I was 18. And I stayed in touch. Today, e-mail would be a great way to stay in touch with all the new contacts you make. It's an easy way to communicate and, best of all, it's free!

It's not important who Mr. X is. What is important is that I met Mr. X when I was 18 years old. You are never too young to start making contacts.

Communication built that relationship for me, just as it will for you. Your Mr. X might be your next-door neighbor or it might be the sister of one of your friends (in which case, of course, it would be Ms. X.) You just never know who your Mr. or Ms. X might be, so treat everyone you meet with respect and great interest. Remember, you can learn something from everyone you meet. As you build your relationships with communication, doors will open, opportunity will knock, and friendships will be made. Your process of "luck" will develop.

You can never keep in touch with too many people. I learned this lesson at an early age from my father, the guy with the Timex. He is the absolute king of correspondence. The man has licked more stamps than anyone on earth. My father was famous for saying, "If you're bored, write a letter." For some reason, this went in one ear and got stuck before it came out the other. I followed his advice, but I wasn't sure what letter writing had to do with my future.

When my father finished college, he drove from his hometown in Delaware to Midland, Texas, to work in the oil fields. The job he had been promised was a position as a "roughneck" on an oil rig. Not only was it the lowest-paying job on the rig, it was also the dirtiest. The roughneck handled the drill pipe as it came in and out of the ground. At day's end, the roughneck was always covered with mud that smelled like week-old shrimp.

Luckily for my dad, the grimy job he was promised had fallen through. Unfortunately, another job, just as grimy, became available two weeks later. In the meantime, my dad looked up a guy in Midland named Toby. Toby was a friend of one of my dad's acquaintances back in Delaware. Toby invited my dad out to lunch with Poppy, one of the other guys in his building. Toby, Poppy, and my dad became friends and continued to have lunch together for several months, until my dad finally got transferred out of the mud and out of the state.

> **"D**on't depend on a rabbit's foot for luck; remember, it didn't work too well for the rabbit."
>
> Anonymous

As you might expect, the three new friends kept in touch by mail for years to come, especially Poppy and my dad. Ironically, they would never see each other in person again. For the next 30 years, all they did was write letters to each other every few months. Thirty years! My dad eventually went to law school, got married, and had three children — which explains how I got here. Poppy, whose first name is really George, moved to Washington, D.C. because his last name just happened to be Bush, and he became President of the United States. True story.

When I was a teenager, I remember my dad telling me about this friend of his in Texas who was becoming quite prominent on the political scene. A few years later, he told me that his friend, George Bush, was the same George Bush that had just been elected Vice President of the United States. Every kid wants to believe their father, but I was having a tough time with this one — until a few years later.

I was in Dallas, Texas, on business. I walked down to the health club at my hotel for a quick workout. The club was swarming with Secret Service agents. I asked one of them what was going on and he told me that Vice President Bush was in town.

"Oh really?" I said. "Do you know where he is? He's a friend of my father and I'd like to say hello." I'm sure the agent thought I was insane. He looked at me and said, "Get a life, kid. I can't tell you where he is."

He didn't have to. I looked down the hall and there he was, Vice President Bush surrounded by ten Secret Service agents. They were heading my way, and as they got closer, my heart started pounding and my knees started knocking. I think I forgot to breathe for a minute. Finally, just as they were about to go by, I thought, "What the heck, I've got nothing to lose here."

So, like an idiot, I yelled, "Vice President Bush."

You would have thought a shot had been fired. The ten Secret Service agents swarmed around the Vice President while two more agents got in my face.

The whole group stopped for a brief second and I assumed that was my cue to continue. "Hi, I'm Chad Foster from Lafayette, Louisiana." Vice President Bush looked up, cracked a smile, and said, "Really? You must be David's son." "Yes sir, I am," I answered as I finally started breathing again. The ten agents with the Vice President backed off. They made room for me as I moved forward to shake hands with Mr. Bush. The Vice President and I had a conversation about our families and our travels, and then went our separate ways.

A week or so later, my father called. He said he was sending me an overnight package containing something he thought I would enjoy. The package arrived the next morning and I opened it immediately. It was a handwritten postcard to my father from George Bush telling my dad that he had met me in Dallas.

Unbelievable! To this day, I'm still amazed. How could a guy as busy as Vice President Bush find time to write a postcard to someone he hadn't seen in 30 years, about some 27-year-old kid he didn't even know? Letter writing was beginning to take on a whole new meaning for me. I guess my dad was right — once again.

George Bush was not a politician by nature. He was a master of communication. George Bush was elected President of the United States in 1988 by the friends and contacts he made, and stayed in touch with, over a 40-year period.

You can never stay in touch with too many people. Fill your address book and then get another one.

In case you're wondering, I wrote a letter of my own to Vice President Bush when I got home. And yes, he wrote me back a few days later.

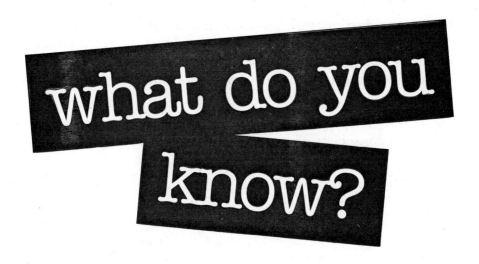

what do you know?

The formula is simple. The more people you meet, the more you learn, and the more interesting you become. Likewise, the more interesting you are, the easier it will be to meet people.

There's just one problem with this picture. Nobody is very interesting when they are born, and the average infant hasn't met many people. So which comes first, the chicken or the egg? If you haven't met many people, how do you become interesting? And if you aren't interesting yet, how do you meet many people? I guess you could just walk out into the street and start introducing yourself to everyone you see, exchange addresses and phone numbers, and tell them you'll be back in touch when you become interesting. I suggest a different approach. I suggest that you work on the "interesting" side of the equation first.

Just how does one become interesting at the ripe old age of 13, 15, or even 18? It's easy — you read everything you can very carefully, you ask a million questions, and you listen. Of the three, reading is probably the easiest to accomplish, because it is the one activity that you have the most control over. The sky's the limit when it comes to available reading material. Just walk into any library and you will have it all right at your fingertips. The Internet is one of your best resources for a wide variety of reading material. It's available, it's convenient and, at school, it's free — my favorite four-letter word.

The secret to becoming well informed is to expand your knowledge on a variety of subjects. It is no longer good enough to know a lot about just one subject. The real world demands that your knowledge be diverse.

The easiest way to achieve this is to read everything you can get your hands on. Read every book you can, both fiction and nonfiction. Read all kinds of magazines, and most importantly, read newspapers. Newspapers are full of current events, and current event knowledge is critical. Current events are a big part of most conversations. Some of your current event knowledge will come from television, and some will come from talking to others, but most will come from the newspaper. Read it today, tomorrow, and every day you possibly can.

If you only read the front page, or just the sports section, you haven't read the newspaper. Every day in life is like a pop quiz on current events. Make sure you do your homework.

I forgot to do my homework one day. I was invited to a television awards event and the day of the event was a busy one for me. I only had time to read the front page of the paper before leaving my house. The front-page story was all about the latest news in Bosnia. I read with great interest about the horrible civil war that was raging there. I didn't have time to read the sports section or any other section of the paper, so I just tossed them into the trash and headed out the door.

When I arrived at the television event, I found myself in line right behind General John Galvin. Not only is General Galvin a retired four-star general, he was also the Special Ambassador to Bosnia at that time.

Thank goodness I read that front-page story. I couldn't wait to talk about Bosnia with General Galvin. I was a little nervous as I prepared to ask the General a question. But before I could get a word out of my mouth, he looked my way and asked about the Atlanta Braves baseball team. All I could think of was the sports section that I didn't read, in my trash can at home.

Do yourself a favor. Read the whole paper. If you don't get the paper at home, you can read it on the Internet every day. So there's really no excuse for not reading the paper every day.

> "Who you know will get your foot in the door.
> What you know will keep your foot out of your mouth."
>
> Cajun Proverb

The process of becoming more interesting is ongoing. It never ends. It continues as you meet new people — as you make new contacts. Every meeting will be an opportunity for new knowledge. The knowledge you gain will ultimately depend on your ability to ask questions. I like to call this your curiosity level. Ray Kroc, the founder of McDonald's, often said, "When you're green, you grow — when you're ripe, you rot." He wanted his employees to understand the importance of seeking new knowledge. The more questions you ask, the more answers you get. Those answers are knowledge, and that knowledge makes you more interesting. The more interesting you are, the more valuable you are to any company in the world. But remember, asking questions is a skill that you have to practice if you want to get good at it. It's just like any skill — shooting a basketball, riding a bike, or playing the piano — the more you practice, the better you get.

Don't be intimidated by people you find yourself in conversation with, regardless of their age, position, wealth, or intellect. Adults enjoy talking to younger people. You can keep a conversation going with anyone just by asking simple questions. And then just listen to the answer to get your idea for your next question. Almost every conversation begins with a question, and no conversation ever ends with one. You can never ask too many questions. Always remember:

1. People like to answer questions. It makes them feel important.
2. People like to talk about themselves, whether they admit it or not.

A couple of years ago, I ran into Arnold Schwarzenegger at the White House. I know he's famous, but I struck up a conversation with him anyway. It went like this:

"Arnold, how long have you been in town?" I asked.

> **"You only learn when you listen. You learn nothing when you talk."**
>
> Anonymous

"Two days only," he answered.

"Where do you go next?" I asked.

"I'm going to Chicago tomorrow," he said.

"What are you going there for?" I asked.

"I'm speaking to high school students about physical fitness," Arnold explained.

"Do you ever get tired of traveling?" I asked.

"Sometimes," he said, "but I enjoy speaking to the students, so traveling is good."

Our conversation went on for less than a minute, but it could have lasted a lot longer. I didn't make a single statement. All I did was ask questions — simple questions.

Every time Arnold answered one of my questions, he gave me an idea for my next question. It's easy, and you can do it. As the conversation gets going, just listen to the other person's answers very carefully. It will be easy to come up with your next question. Keep your questions simple:

- Where are you from?
- How long have you lived here?
- Where do you work?
- Do you like your job?
- What are your hobbies?

Remember, older people are anxious to talk to younger people. They don't expect your questions to be complex or complicated. This isn't about testing your intelligence; it's about learning to communicate. Try it on one of your friends' parents. Try it on one of your parents' friends. These will be the easiest adults to talk to since you already know them. Practice on them until you are comfortable with the process, then try it on a few people you don't know very well. Like anything else, the more you practice, the easier it becomes.

Before I let the Arnold Schwarzenegger story end, I think there is something you should know. Arnold was at the White House because he was chairman of the President's Council on Physical Fitness and Sports. He spent an entire year traveling the country to speak to students about the importance of physical fitness. Arnold's message is important, but what's really cool is that a guy who gets paid millions for a few weeks on a movie set would take a year out of his schedule to speak to students. That's impressive. Arnold Schwarzenegger believes in young people.

Speaking of young people, I saw a survey that said teenagers today are doomed to fail. The survey also said that most young people are on track to be brain-dead adults. The survey blamed too much TV and too many video games. It even called teenagers a bunch of "Nintendo Heads."

I think the survey might be brain-dead. I say play your Nintendo and watch your TV. But, like anything else, do it in moderation — a little TV, a little Nintendo, a little homework, a little recreation, a little music, a little time on the phone, a little reading, a little writing, a little time with your girlfriend or boyfriend, a little time on the computer, a little time at the mall, a little time with the parents, etc. There is time to do it all, and the more you do, the more interesting you will be.

Maybe you have heard of Bill Gates. Computers have always been his passion, and I'm sure that included computer games. He went on to start a company called Microsoft and today, this "Nintendo Head" is worth $100 billion. I wonder what the guy who wrote the survey is worth.

Do you think the man who started MTV came up with the idea by not watching TV?

The
Future

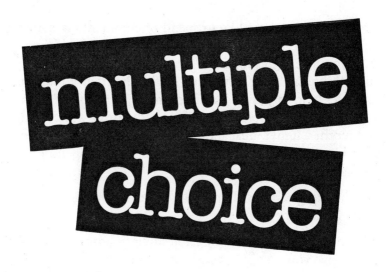

multiple choice

At some point, we all need money. Some of you will need more than others, some of you will have more than you need, and some of you will never have enough.

Where will your money come from? By now you probably know that it doesn't grow on trees. I'm sure your parents have reminded you of this more than a few times. Assuming there's no money tree in your backyard, your money can come from four places: you will either earn it, inherit it, marry it, or steal it. Since stealing it is illegal, marrying it is unlikely, and inheriting it takes forever, it is safe to say that 99 percent of you will have to earn your money. Sorry to deliver the bad news.

Having been dealt that dose of reality, the real question now is, "How will you earn it?"

Before we address that question, let's consider another one: "When will you earn it?" This one's a little easier to answer. Most of you will earn it 40 hours a week, for 50 weeks each year, between the ages of 22 and 65. We're talking about 86,000 hours of your life!

Since most of us don't like to spend one hour doing something we don't enjoy, I'm sure you can see the importance of choosing the right job. If you love your job, life is great. On the other hand, if you hate your job, life is a drag. Trust me: 86,000 hours is a long time to be miserable. Not only that, but if you hate your job 8–10 hours every day, it's virtually impossible to come home from work and be a very good mother, father, husband, or wife. Your choice of careers is one of the biggest decisions you will ever make — and no one else can make it for you.

Now the big questions: How will you earn your money? What will you do for a living?

Just think of this as a multiple-choice question on a test. To help you out, I'll give you all of the wrong answers first.

Wrong Answer #1
I want to be a lawyer because my mother is a lawyer.
or
I want to be a teacher because my father is a teacher.

First, understand that I am not picking on lawyers and teachers. Both are respectable and admirable professions. I am simply using them as examples. This message applies to all professions.

Second, if your parents are lawyers or teachers, they may be very good ones. But that doesn't mean you will be good at either profession. Nor does it mean that you will be happy with either of those careers. On the other hand, having a parent who is a lawyer or a teacher doesn't mean that you'll be unhappy or unsuccessful with those careers either.

The point is, having parents who are teachers and lawyers doesn't mean anything about your future career. It simply means that you have parents who are teachers and lawyers. A lot of people make the mistake of choosing the same career as one of their parents. Watch out. This could be an 86,000-hour mistake.

There are some things in life that you will inherit from your parents, like the color of your eyes or the size of your nose. These are things you can't control. The career you choose is not inherited. This is something you can, and should, control.

Wrong Answer #2
I want a job that will make me rich.

What is rich anyway? This is something you have to figure out for yourself. If rich is money, when is enough really enough? Will $1 million be enough, or will you need $10 million? Be careful. The money chase can be dangerous, much like a roller coaster at the amusement park. Once you get on, you can't get off, and when you finally do stop, sometimes the ride has made you so sick it wasn't really worth it.

> **"M**oney doesn't always bring happiness. People with 10 million dollars don't seem any happier than people with 9 million dollars."**
>
> Hobart Brown

Whether you are 14, 16, or 60, everybody has the same basic needs: health and happiness. Money can't buy either one. Don't miss the message here. There is absolutely nothing wrong with money. I kind of like it myself. But remember, money cannot make you happy. Money has never made anyone happy. I have more miserable, rich friends than you can count. Unfortunately, some people think that money makes the world go around. I've had a few friends who felt this way. Bigger houses, more cars, expensive clothes, etc. Their worlds went around and around until they were spinning out of control. A couple of my friends couldn't stop the spinning, so they stopped something else — their lives. The fast lane finally did them in. One of them had a heart attack. The other one stuck a gun in his mouth and blew his brains out.

Money can and should be the *result* of your work, but money should never be the *reason* for your work.

Wrong Answer #3
I want to be famous.

As with money, there's absolutely nothing wrong with fame — as long as it is the result of your work and never the reason for it. It is possible to be famous and happy, but fame cannot make you happy. I wish you could ask Marilyn Monroe, Elvis Presley, or Kurt Cobain if fame made them happy. Unfortunately, they all checked out early.

Choosing a job is a huge decision. Some estimates say that 75 percent of all workers are dissatisfied with their jobs. That's a scary thought.

The average worker now changes careers — not just jobs, but careers — three to four times before retirement.

When it came to choosing a career, I was very fortunate. I worked in the same industry, with the same people, for 13 years. As those 13 years flew by, I watched too many of my friends hate their jobs, change their jobs, and not have jobs. It was only after I stopped working that I began to understand why my 13-year career was so incredible. It's simple. I loved my job. You see, if you love your job life is incredible.

Since I gave you all the wrong answers, I might as well give you the right answers, too. I wish I'd had these answers when I was a teenager.

Right Answer #1
I am choosing a career because I have the natural talents to do the job.

Every one of you is blessed with natural talents. They are innate. You are born with them and you are stuck with them, whether you like it or not. Shaquille O'Neal's natural talent is basketball. Shania Twain's natural talent is music. I have a feeling they like the natural talents they got stuck with.

When you start working, it's important to do something that uses your natural talents. The bad news is that your natural talents are not listed on your birth certificate, so some of you may not know what they are. The good news is that the next chapter will show you how to uncover your natural talents.

Right Answer #2
I am choosing a career that I have tried.

You know how you feel about school because you've tried it. You know how you feel about MTV because you've watched it. You know how you feel about your parents because you've tried them. Obviously, the odds of liking your job are much better if you've tried it. Unfortunately, most people don't try enough jobs before they have to choose one. Fortunately, one of the next chapters is all about trying jobs.

Right Answer #3
I am choosing a career that will allow me to pay my bills, save some money, and still maintain the quality of life I need.

This is a tough one for some young people to understand. Society is always telling you how important money is, and now I'm stepping up and telling you it just isn't true. You will probably have to figure this one out for yourself. As you go about this, though, remember my friend who blew his brains out. He was confused. He thought money made the world go around.

On the subject of money, I can promise you this:

A. If you do what you love, the money will follow.

B. Money is only good for two things:

    1. To provide you with all the material things you need — but not necessarily all the material things you want.

    2. To do things for others who may be less fortunate than you.

This should be the easiest test you've ever taken. All the answers have been provided.

Remember, it's 86,000 hours of your life.

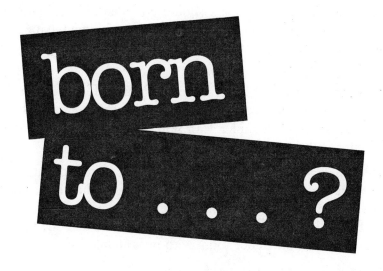

born to . . . ?

Have you ever met people who hate their jobs? Have you ever wondered why this happens? Maybe those people weren't cut out for their jobs. Maybe their jobs weren't cut out for them.

I've often heard the term "natural-born" salesperson, and I've read about many "gifted" musicians. What do these words "natural" and "gifted" mean? The "gifts" that we refer to are not Christmas gifts; they are more like birthday gifts. You get them the day you are born. These are the only gifts you don't write thank-you notes for. They are innate, meaning that you are born with them. These innate gifts are your aptitudes.

Aptitudes are defined as natural talents and special abilities for doing, or learning to do, certain kinds of things easily and quickly.

I always thought that natural talents referred only to physical abilities, like swimming or catching a baseball. That's probably why I had such a huge fight with my parents when I was 15. They wanted me to drive five hours to Houston, Texas, for two days of testing. They explained something about a test that would reveal my natural aptitudes and talents. They said that after I took the tests, the testing company could tell me what I should do when I finished school. I didn't like it when people told me what to do with my life for free, so you can imagine how I felt about some testing company getting paid to tell me what to do.

Of course, my parents never checked with me before they scheduled these tests. Nor did they have the common sense to schedule them during the week, so I could at least skip two days of school. Not only that, but they sent me to take the tests on my birthday!

So, we fought — I screamed; they won — and off to Houston I went. I didn't want to go. I didn't want to take the tests when I arrived. And I sure didn't want to sit in a conference room two days later, with my parents, to discuss my results. But I did go, I did take the tests, and I did sit in that conference room with my parents.

Why? Because I was a great kid.

Are you kidding? I was a pain in the butt! The only reason I went to Houston and took those tests was that I grew up in a home that was probably much like yours. Parents say it, and kids do it. Parents always think they know what is best for their kids. Sometimes they do. Sometimes they don't. This time they did.

When I left Houston, I put the cassette tape containing my aptitude test results in the glove compartment of my car, where it sat for two years. When I sold that car, I took the tape out of that glove compartment and put it in the glove compartment of my new car, where it sat for four more years. I'm not even sure why I kept the stupid tape. I didn't care to listen to my test results in person, so I wasn't about to listen to them on tape. But, two more cars, two more glove compartments, and eight years later, I finally listened to the tape. I was 30 by this time, so 15 years had passed since I took that aptitude test. By then, I had been in business for 10 years, so I had a pretty good idea of what my aptitudes might be. I just listened to the tape to see if those guys at the testing lab had a clue.

As I rode down the highway listening to my results, I felt like I was in the movie *Back to the Future*. The guy on the tape was explaining my test scores and the types of careers my aptitudes were best suited for. When the tape was over, I ejected it to take a closer look. I was sure that someone had switched tapes on me. I couldn't believe that this was the tape they had given me 15 years earlier. I played the tape one more time and thought I was losing my mind. Based on my aptitudes, those guys in Houston had predicted my future so accurately that it was scary. They warned that I would be bored with school. So bored, they said, that I might not stick around long enough to finish. They knew I wouldn't work for a big corporation and that I'd thrive on the flexibility of working with a small company. They were sure I had a need to travel and to constantly meet new people. They predicted my strengths would be in sales and marketing. All of this when I was 15 years old! I had to laugh at myself for being such a pain when I took the test.

A big part of succeeding and being happy in life is working in a career that uses your natural abilities. An aptitude test can help you make this happen.

Take advantage of this opportunity to uncover your natural talents. It can be critical in your search to choose a career that you will find rewarding and that you will be good at. Also, if you don't use the aptitudes that you possess, you might find yourself very frustrated later in life.

Understanding your aptitudes will also be helpful as you search for your passion. Sometimes your job doesn't use all of your aptitudes. This is where your passion comes in.

You can't pass or fail an aptitude test. You shouldn't even think of it as a test. It's just information that can do nothing but help you. There are no good or bad scores. The purpose of the test is to uncover your natural aptitudes and then to understand how they all fit together.

If you want to know more about aptitude tests, check with your guidance counselor at school or do a search on the Internet.

try it . . . . you might hate it

Once you understand your aptitudes and natural talents, you will have a pretty good idea of the general career direction that you should follow. Now you can start to consider a few jobs that match your aptitudes. This isn't the time to pick your "job for life," but it is a good time to start thinking about it. The more time you have to think, the better your chances are of making the right choice. Remember, it's not where you start your journey, it's when you start that makes all the difference in the world.

Whatever your age, stop for a minute and consider this question: What do you want to do when you get out of school? Chances are you've heard this question before. Often, it comes from an adult who really doesn't care about the answer but just can't think of anything else to say. Maybe someone should write a book that teaches adults how to talk to young people.

So what do you want to do? Most teenagers have no clue, and that's okay.

In a recent study, groups of teenagers were asked what they wanted to be when they got out of school. The most common answer? "I want to be employed."

Let's agree on one thing. Your ultimate goal is to choose a career that you will enjoy and a job that you will be good at. You probably won't make that final career choice until you are out of school. But now is the time to prepare. *Live* for today, *plan* for tomorrow.

As you probably know, there's a lot more to a job than showing up in the morning and leaving at the end of the day. The work environment can be difficult to adjust to, especially if you've never tried it. Your job is something you are going to deal with five days a week for most of your life. There's nothing better than loving your job, and there's nothing worse than hating it. Don't forget, it's 86,000 hours of your life.

You test-drive a car before you buy it. You try on clothes before you buy them. Why would anyone with half a brain choose a career she hasn't tried? You don't need to pick a career while you're still in school, but it is a good idea to test-drive a few.

If someone told you that fried worms tasted great, would you agree to eat worms five times a week for the rest of your life before you tried them? I hope not.

WARNING: Choosing the wrong job will be hazardous to your health. It could be worse than eating fried worms.

So how do you try a job in a career that you haven't even chosen? You don't try one job, you try several. That way, when the time comes to choose a full-time career, you will speak from experience. You will know what fried worms taste like, and if you don't like them, you won't eat them for 86,000 hours of your life. You can make an intelligent career choice based on what you know you are good at (natural aptitudes), combined with what you have tried.

We are talking internships here. Webster's dictionary defines an intern as "a student who is getting practical experience under the guidance of an experienced worker." Most people think internships are only for college and university students. Most people are clueless. Why wait until you've spent three or four years in post-secondary school and tons of money on tuition to start figuring out which jobs you like and which you don't? It doesn't make much sense to me.

Internships don't have to be full-time. They can be summer-long, week-long, or just for a day. The length of your internship is not what's important.

What you learn and who you meet while you're there are what's most critical. Regardless of length, internships will give you a sneak preview of the jobs you think you might like. You will have a chance to see the jobs from the inside, and that way, you will see the good, the bad, and the ugly. If the bad and ugly outweigh the good, then that's one career you can scratch off your list.

When should you start your sneak previews? As soon as you can, and long before college. The more internships you try, the more you will know about what you might like to do later in life. More important, though, internships will help you decide what not to do when you get out of school.

Use your summers wisely. Don't get me wrong. I don't think you should work your summers away. Hanging out is part of growing up. It's your right to hang out and do nothing every once in awhile. But just as hanging out is one of your rights, preparing for tomorrow is one of your responsibilities. Commit a few days each summer to checking out jobs. A couple of days here, a few hours there. Work for free. That way, if you like what you're doing, you can extend your stay; if you hate the place, you can hit the road. The math here is simple: three or four sneak previews each summer during high school and you've looked at 12 to 16 careers. That way, when you meet with the guidance counselors at school, you can do the talking and they can do the listening. It can't help but help.

How will you know which internships to do? Rumor has it that there are 20,000 different jobs to be had. So I guess your choice of internships will be limited to 20,000. That might seem a little overwhelming. Not a problem. All you need to do is go back and review your natural aptitudes and interests. Here's where you figure out how they

> **"If you wake up tomorrow and believe that you can trade a degree for success, go back to sleep — it was just a bad dream."**
>
> Kramer

all fit together. If your aptitudes are strong in the field of medicine, and you love animals, you might want to do an internship with your local veterinarian. On the other hand, if you have a great interest in plants and animals, but you know you're allergic to hard work, don't even dream of interning on a farm. Consider your natural talents and what you like to do most. Put them together and you'll know where to go.

This is where the easy part starts. Once you know which internships you want, just walk in and ask. It's not hard to do. Here's how it works.

So you think you want to be a lawyer and you want a sneak preview of that job this summer? This one's easy. Almost everyone knows a lawyer. For that matter, almost everyone *is* a lawyer (but that's a later chapter).

Odds are, your parents will know at least one lawyer. Get the phone number from your parents so that you can call the lawyer and ask if you can spend a couple of days at his or her office. Tell the lawyer that you are thinking about a career in law. If you are not totally comfortable making that initial call, a letter might be easier:

Dear Mr. Jackson,

My parents, David and Sarah Thompson, have told me that you are an excellent lawyer. I am 16 years old and I am considering a career in law. I would like to spend a day or two working in your office this summer so that I can get an inside look at what lawyers really do. I don't need to be paid and my schedule is flexible. I will call you next week to see if this might be possible.

Thank you,
Wendy Thompson

A week later, follow your letter with a call and get ready to go to work. I can't imagine anyone who wouldn't say yes. Not only will most adults say yes, but they will be impressed by a teenager who cares enough about his own future to ask for help.

Repeat this process for each career you are interested in. Don't forget who your best resources are — some of your friends' parents or some of your parents' friends. As always, they will be the easiest to approach and the most willing to help. But feel free to ask anyone to let you do an internship at their company. Before I wrote this chapter, I asked 50 people what they would say if a teenager called them for an internship. They all said yes. Nobody said no. If someone does say no to your request, write it off as experience and go on to the next person. Whatever you do, don't let it discourage you.

Besides the obvious, there are many benefits to these mini-internships or sneak previews. In most cases, you will be working with adults. This will give you an opportunity to make more contacts. Remember *"the 'meet' of the matter"* chapter? Since these new contacts will be in an industry of interest to you, they are even more valuable. Remember David Brantley, the guy I built the multimillion-dollar company with? I first met him while I was doing an internship when I was 15. You just never know.

Don't forget to fill that address book. Get a business card from everyone you meet and then stay in touch with them. These days, that won't be too hard since so many people have an e-mail address. Stay in touch with everyone you meet.

The days of trading a degree for the perfect job are over. There just aren't enough good jobs to go around anymore. Here's what's happening out in the real world. In just three years, IBM laid off 85,000 associates, AT&T laid off 83,000 employees, General Motors laid off 74,000 workers, and Sears laid off 50,000 more.

These people weren't laid off for poor performance. They were let go because they weren't needed anymore. When you hit the real world, a degree will be a big help. But you'll also need a little something extra to get your foot in the door and to open that window of opportunity — something to separate you from everyone else. Your contacts will be that little something extra. People make people successful.

The day will come when you're out on the streets, pounding the pavement, looking for your dream job. It might be hard to think that far ahead, but the work skills you develop now will be critical. I saw an interesting study in the newspaper recently. It was done to see how part-time work affected high school students.

These are the results:

1. High school students who work part-time usually make more money later in life than students who don't work during school.

2. High school seniors who work 20 hours per week are expected to earn 20 percent more after college or university than those students who don't work during high school.

In another study, Paul Barton with the Educational Testing Service found that students who work up to 20 hours per week actually have better grades than those who don't work at all. Paul Barton should know, since his company developed the Scholastic Aptitude Test (SAT).

The bottom line? Part-time jobs can ease your transition into the workplace. These jobs will help you improve your knowledge of the job market, gain some workplace skills, and make valuable contacts. Almost every successful person I have ever met worked part-time as a teenager.

As you finish each sneak preview or part-time job, take a break to evaluate. If you didn't like what you saw, then maybe that's not the job for you. At least you learned something. It was time well spent.

On the other hand, if you thought the job was cool, then you can consider it as one of your options when choosing a career. Again, you have learned something and your time was well spent. Maybe a few more days at a similar job, but with a different company, would be a good idea.

Don't forget to write a note of thanks to the person who hired you, and be sure to stay in touch with all of the people you worked with. These are the men and women who will help you achieve your goals later in life.

A few days each summer is a small price to pay. Your sneak previews will make a huge difference when you enter the real world.

out of the ordinary

I don't get it. Why does everyone want to be a lawyer or a doctor? Don't they know they have a thousand other choices? Correction: make that 20,000 other choices.

Maybe they don't know because maybe nobody told them. When I was in school, everyone who was really smart went to medical school. The people who didn't know what they wanted to do went to law school. We ended up with a bunch of really smart doctors — some happy, some not — and a pile of unhappy, confused lawyers. The point is that many times people don't consider all of their options when choosing a career. That's usually because they don't know what all of their options are. If there really are 20,000 different jobs to be had, how many of those 20,000 do you think you are familiar with? Just think of how many great careers you have never even heard of. Whatever you do, don't make an 86,000-hour decision before you consider all of your options, or at least as many as you possibly can.

I was probably supposed to be a lawyer myself. My grandfather was a lawyer and so was my father. I probably had "lawyer" tattooed on my forehead when I was born. It wasn't easy convincing some people that I wasn't going to be a lawyer.

After I had been in the business of building tennis courts and playgrounds for several years, I ran into a woman from my hometown. Her name is Mary and she was married to a doctor. Mary stopped me at a restaurant and asked what I had been doing lately. I told her I was in the tennis court and playground business, to which she immediately responded, "You're still doing that?" I guess she thought I had chosen a career that had little or no future. After all, I wasn't a lawyer like my dad, and I wasn't a doctor like her husband. Anyway, since our business had been at a multimillion-dollar level for several years, I had to throw a little sarcasm her way. I said, "Yes ma'am, I'm still doing that." Then I asked, "By the way, Mary, how is your husband, Bob?" She said he was fine and that he was at the hospital. I asked her if he was sick, and she said, "No, he's seeing patients." I couldn't resist. I asked, "Really, is he *still* a doctor?"

There are lots of great jobs you might not have thought of. The best way to find out about them is to ask the people you meet what kind of work they do. You will probably meet several people who do something you've never heard of. When this happens, ask them to tell you more about their jobs. Remember, people love to talk about themselves, and that includes their jobs. Don't forget to ask them for a business card and then be sure to stay in touch with them. People make people successful.

Maybe you will meet someone who loves music and shopping for clothes. That sounds like a typical teenager to me, but maybe it's not. Maybe this *was* a teenager a few years ago who wanted a job that would include her two favorite interests — music and clothes. Maybe it's someone like my friend Claudia, in Nashville, Tennessee. She is a wardrobe stylist. She picks out clothes for people like Garth Brooks, Reba McIntyre, and Shania Twain to wear on music videos. Claudia works for herself, travels around the country, hangs out with music stars, and does what she loves. What more could you ask?

You *should* ask, "How does one get there from here?"

Great question. Watch tons of music videos and do a lot of window shopping. A part-time job in retail fashion during high school wouldn't hurt either. Don't forget a short internship with a local fashion consultant. Follow that up with a Fashion Merchandising major in college. Blast out of school with your degree and grab a couple of years' experience in retail fashion. Now you're set. Just call on some of your contacts to open a few doors and you're on your way. You did remember to make lots of contacts along the way, didn't you? If not, take two Tylenol and go back to *"the 'meet' of the matter"* chapter.

There are hundreds of unusual jobs like this. Unfortunately, you can't always learn about them at school. But if you meet enough people and ask enough questions, you'll eventually get the answers you're looking for. When you meet people who have jobs that sound cool, don't let them get away before you pick their brain and learn all you can. They will be flattered, and when people are flattered they will go out of their way to help you. I tried this myself and came up with a few ideas that aren't your everyday "bore me to death, put me to sleep" kind of jobs. If these jobs do put you to sleep, maybe you should be a lawyer or a doctor. By the way, there's nothing wrong with being a lawyer or a doctor, but there is a lot wrong with not considering all of your options.

You will notice that nothing is said about how much any of these jobs pay. Remember: do what you love and the money will follow.

Check these out:

WEDDING PHOTOGRAPHER

If taking pictures floats your boat, this might be the ticket for you. Most weddings are on Friday or Saturday, which leaves the rest of the week to you. A good photographer can work anywhere, so travel could be a big part of the job. Your ability to sell will also be important, since you'll have to sell your services to the bride and her family.

How to Get There from Here:

Wedding photographer Denis Reggie says that as a teenager, he shot as many people as he could — with a camera, of course. Read up on wedding photography and attend seminars in your area. Study business in school with an emphasis on sales and marketing. Do an internship with a good wedding photographer as soon as you can. Denis's advice should be good His clients include Arnold Schwarzenegger, John F. Kennedy, Jr., and Mariah Carey.

FOOD STYLIST

Food stylists are not people who look very stylish when they eat In fact, food stylist Patti Thursby says she rarely has time to eat as she flies coast to coast working with companies like Hardee's, Arby's, and Coca-Cola. Her job is to arrange food before it is photographed for national TV ads. Before I met Patti, I didn't even know there was such a job. I always thought the food in the pictures was fake.

How to Get There from Here:

Don't change the channel when the commercials come on. This is your chance to see some of the world's best work. It's an art, so pay close attention to detail. Intern or work part-time before college with an advertising agency that handles major food clients. College courses should include home economics, food science, and art. If you get this job, don't go to work hungry. You get paid to arrange the food, not to eat it.

MOVIE CRITIC

How can they even call this a job? Sit back, have some popcorn, and wash it down with a Coke. See a movie today and write a review of it tomorrow. Most TV stations and newspapers hire movie critics. If you're intrigued with Hollywood and you like to write, this might be just the thing for you.

How to Get There from Here:

This job is basically opinion and style. Opinion is easy, because everyone has one. Good style is like a good idea: it's almost always borrowed, at least until you develop your own. See lots of movies and read lots of reviews. Write your own review of a movie, then compare it to a professional review. Consider an internship at your local paper. Make it your business to get to know the movie critic. Once you've done that, ask him or her for help. Maybe your school paper could use a movie critic. That was my idea, but you're welcome to borrow it.

RETAIL BUYER

This is the next best thing to being born rich. You get to go shopping with someone else's money. Almost every store has a buyer: record stores, clothing stores, bike stores, etc. Buyers get to travel here and there as they pick and choose their products. Of course, what you buy is expected to sell, so there's a little more to it than just buying what you like. You have to have a feel for what the customer wants. A "50% off" sale is usually a sign of a buyer who missed the boat.

How to Get There from Here:

Work part-time in retail as a teenager, then work full-time in retail after school. Know your product, get a feel for your customer's tastes, and throw in a business degree for good luck. Don't forget to intern with a buyer if you can.

TRAVELING NURSE

Remember, nurses can be male or female. If you are interested in medicine and want to travel, pack your bags and get ready to go. Traveling nurses move from city to city, usually every 13 weeks. It's part of the deal and it's a great opportunity to meet lots of people. Your housing, salary, and medical benefits are provided by the company you work for. All you have to do is show up for work and be a tourist in your free time.

How to Get There from Here:

This one's pretty basic. You will need a nursing degree plus two years of experience at a hospital. A sneak preview of nursing while you're in high school wouldn't be a bad idea either.

DISC JOCKEY

If you love to talk and don't like listening to anyone talk back, this might be the job for you. It's not for you, though, if you often find yourself at a loss for words. You won't have to be quick on your feet, but being quick with your tongue is essential. Steve McCoy, one of the top disc jockeys in Atlanta, Georgia, says, "You have to sound like you're in the car with your listener when you talk into that microphone." He should know. He's one of the best in the business.

How to Get There from Here:

First, understand that it's not all about music. Business sense and management skills both play a role. During high school, find a radio station that fits your taste and beg for an internship. Your next job is to become the disc jockey's best friend. Ask lots of questions and listen carefully to the answers. Radio and Television Communication is the best college major. Plan for tomorrow. Pick a school that has its own radio station.

LOTTERY WINNER

You wish. That's okay, so do I!

These are just a few careers you may not have thought of. There are hundreds of others, and all you have to do to discover them is meet people, ask questions, and listen closely — in that order.

P.S. If you work part-time, make sure that you get more than a check out of the experience. Learn the skills of the people working around you — assistant managers, managers, marketing people, customer service, etc. The skills that make these people good at what they do are the same skills that you will need as you continue your journey to success. Don't pass up an opportunity to learn from those people you work with at your part-time job. Just as important, don't pass up an opportunity to meet and get to know all of the people you work with at your part-time job. That's right — even if you're flipping burgers. You just never know where those people will be in a few years when you are looking for a full-time job.

Speaking of flipping burgers. McDonald's is a great place to work part-time as a teenager. You might not know this, but a lot of the men and women who own McDonald's franchises around the country that make millions of dollars started out flipping burgers part-time as a teenager. Don't ever think flipping burgers or making fries is a dead-end job. The opportunities within a great company like McDonald's are endless. McDonald's offers high-paying jobs in marketing, management, construction, real estate, and advertising — not to mention opportunities to own your own McDonald's store(s). McDonald's is a great place to learn and practice the people skills and communication skills you will need to succeed in any career. How do I know this? I had the pleasure of working with the folks at McDonald's for seven years during which time we installed my playground surface on 3,000 McDonald's Playlands.

Make the most of your part-time work experience.

Take It or Leave It

dream on

Have you ever had a dream? I'm not talking about the kind you have at night that you can't remember when you wake up. And I'm definitely not talking about Saturday mornings, when you're trying to sleep and you hear your mother yelling at you to wake up and clean your room. That's not a dream — that's a nightmare. I know the feeling.

Haven't you ever dreamed of being a movie star or a professional athlete or the president of some huge international company? Or how about doing something extraordinary, like finding a cure for AIDS or cancer?

I hope you have, because all great ideas and all remarkable accomplishments start as dreams. Dreams inspire action.

Perhaps the most famous dream ever had was that of Dr. Martin Luther King, Jr. in 1963. His dream was that black people and white people would learn to live and work together in peace. This was no small dream. He believed so strongly in this dream that he was willing to risk his life for it. In fact, he gave his life for his dream. As you know, Dr. King was killed by an assassin in 1968. But as a result of his dream, progress has been made and the world is a better place.

> **"T**o avoid criticism:
> do nothing,
> say nothing,
> be nothing."
>
> Elbert Hubbard

But we still have a long, long way to go. Racism and discrimination of all kinds are some of the most serious problems we face in America today. If we want to correct these horrible wrongs, we are going to need some help from your generation.

Make sure you treat everyone you meet like a human being, because that's what we all are. Being white doesn't make you any better than if you are black. Being rich doesn't make you any better than if you are poor. And being thin doesn't make you any better than if you are overweight. The success of your generation depends on tolerance of all people. Don't put up with racism or any kind of discrimination.

Like Dr. King, if you have a dream you must pursue it. You must always believe that your dream can come true.

Is it possible for a boy who was raised on a peanut farm to grow up to be President of the United States? Jimmy Carter thought so. Is it possible for a boy from Shelbina, Missouri (population 2,000), to start his own company and become one of the richest men in the U.S.? Sam Walton thought so, and he called his company Wal-Mart. Is it possible that Sandy Day, who was roping cattle in Arizona at the age of nine, could grow up to be Justice Sandra Day O'Connor on the United States Supreme Court? Yes it is.

Dreams do come true, so make sure you pursue your dreams — even if they seem far-fetched.

Here's what happens when you do pursue your dreams. Sometimes that ultimate dream does come true. But even if your ultimate dream does not come true, as you pursue your dreams other doors will open and other opportunities will present themselves. On the other hand, if you don't pursue your dreams, or even worse, if you let someone talk you out of your dreams, then those other doors won't open and those opportunities won't be there.

So starting today, no matter what your dream might be — no matter how far-fetched — pursue it with all your heart and soul. Make sure you do something every single day to pursue your dream and just as important, start telling everybody you know about your dream. Tell your friends, your classmates, your teachers, your parents, and every new person you meet. If you want your dream to come true, you are going to need some help. The more people you tell about your dream, the more help you will get. On the other hand, if you don't tell anyone about your dream you won't get any help. People can't help you if they don't know what your dream is.

Unfortunately, too many people don't follow their dreams. In many cases, they let someone else convince them that their dreams won't come true. Don't make this mistake. If you have a dream or a special idea, pursue it. Don't let it get away. Even if someone else thinks your dream is stupid or a waste of time, pursue it until it comes true, or at least until you're absolutely sure that it wasn't meant to be. That still doesn't mean it was stupid or a waste of time.

Years ago, a man had an idea about a new toy for kids. It looked like an oversized skinny donut and was made of plastic. The man thought kids would twirl this plastic ring around their waists by swinging their hips. I'm sure most people thought it was a crazy, far-fetched idea, but not the man with the idea. He pursued his dream and called his new toy the Hula Hoop.

A few years ago, while I was in the Bahamas, my fishing guide pointed out one of the most beautiful islands I had ever seen. The water was crystal clear and the beaches were outstanding. There was only one hotel on this island, a huge place overlooking the sea of Abaco on one side and the Atlantic Ocean on the other. I asked my guide to take me to the island so I could check it out. He explained to me that what I thought was a hotel was actually someone's home. He went on to tell me that the entire island was owned by one man — the guy who invented the Hula Hoop. One little idea, one great big island.

Dreams do come true.

All the great dreams haven't been dreamed and all the great ideas haven't been had. Furthermore, great ideas are not restricted to one per person. Thomas Edison invented the record player. Obviously, this was a monumental achievement. Without records, there would be no cassettes and no CDs; in which case, there would be no Sony

Walkman, or, heaven forbid, no Sony Discman. Maybe we should celebrate a Thomas Edison day.

But Thomas Edison didn't stop there. He went on to pursue two more unbelievable ideas. One was a little plug that stuck in your ear. Today we call this a hearing aid. And finally, Thomas Edison is the man who made it possible for you to walk the streets at night, drive home in the dark, and sneak into your house without knocking over the kitchen table. Thomas Edison invented the light bulb.

These would be amazing accomplishments for anyone to achieve over the course of a lifetime. Time out. Listen carefully. Thomas Edison invented the record player, the hearing aid, and the light bulb all in one year. Think big. Don't let anyone tell you that your thoughts must walk before they can run just because you are a teenager. A good idea is a good idea, whether it comes from someone 14, or someone 40. A 16-year-old's dream is just as good as a 60-year-old's. Many of you will live tomorrow what you dream today. Your dream is yours; don't let anyone take it away from you.

When I was a teenager, I had a friend named Mark Prudhomme. I often joined his family for lunch on Sundays. Lunch at my house was great on Saturdays, but Sunday lunch usually meant leftovers, so the Prudhomme meal was more appealing.

Almost every time I arrived at the Prudhommes' I saw the same thing. Mark's younger brother, Billy, would be standing in the backyard juggling whatever he could get his hands on: tennis balls, lemons, eggs, etc. You see, Billy Prudhomme had a dream, totally far-fetched in the opinion of most people. He wanted to be a professional juggler. Now I'll admit, that's a pretty far-fetched dream. But that was Billy's dream.

One day while I was at the Prudhomme's house for lunch, Billy's mom opened the back door and called out, "Billy, come in for lunch." When Billy got inside, his mother looked over at him and said, "Billy, you know you can't just stand around and juggle for the rest of your life."

I never forgot what Billy's mother said. You see, Billy was in the backyard juggling because that was his dream, even though it was pretty far-fetched. And there was his mother, right at the back door, trying to talk him out of it.

I never forgot Billy's mother's words. And I didn't see my friend Billy again, until 15 years later. I was on a cruise ship in the Caribbean. The cruise started in Miami and sailed to the ports of St. Thomas,

San Juan, Cancun, and the Bahamas. One of the greatest things about a cruise is the entertainment on board — magicians, comedians, dancers, and others.

The first night of the cruise, I walked into the ship's Grand Ballroom for that night's entertainment. That ballroom was the size of a high school gym. There must have been 1,500 people in that ballroom. As the lights went down, the Master of Ceremonies grabbed the microphone and announced to the crowd, "Good evening, passengers. We are happy to have you aboard the cruise this week. Tonight, we have a special guest entertainer. He's back by popular demand. Please help me welcome world-famous juggler, Billy Prudhomme."

My friend Billy walked out onto that stage and I swear I almost wet my pants! He proceeded to put on a show that was absolutely incredible. For the next 30 minutes, he juggled, told jokes, and had the crowd laughing so hard they were almost crying. That's impressive. If you have ever been on a cruise you know that the average age passenger on a cruise ship is about 94!

After his show, Billy came off stage to say hello to me. Remember, I hadn't seen him in 15 years. In fact, I hadn't seen him since I was at his house the day his mother was trying to talk him out of his far-fetched dream.

After his performance, Billy hung around with me on the ship for the next five days. On the last night of the cruise, Billy had to work again. He put on another show, this time for 15 minutes. He juggled, told jokes, and the crowd went crazy. So, if I have my math right here, Billy works 30 minutes the first night of the cruise and then comes back on stage and works 15 minutes the last night of the cruise. My friend Billy works 45 minutes a week! And for that, he gets paid several thousand dollars.

I think it's pretty cool that Billy gets to travel around the world on a cruise ship. And I also think it's great that he makes all that money. But in my opinion, the most important thing about my friend Billy Prudhomme is that every day when he gets up and goes to work, he loves what he does for a living.

You see, if you like your job — if you like the work you do — life is great. In fact, life is pretty incredible. But, if you hate your job — if you hate the career you choose — life is a total drag. And here's why. Remember, your career is going to last about 86,000 hours. Hating your job is a drag because if you go to work and hate your job for 8–10 hours every day, it's impossible to come home at night and be any kind of mother, father, husband, or wife. Make sure you choose the right career. Dreams are a big part of choosing a job you will like.

Why does Billy Prudhomme get to do what he loves, travel around the world, and make great money? Because he did not let an adult talk him out of his far-fetched dream when he was a teenager.

Whenever I think of Billy and all of his success, it reminds me of his mother, standing at the back door of his house many years ago, saying "Billy, you know you just can't stand around and juggle for the rest of your life."

Actually, the more I think about it, I realize that Billy's mother was right. Billy can't stand around and juggle for the rest of his life. He can only juggle for 45 minutes a week.

Someone brilliant once said, "It is far better to have tried and failed than to never have tried at all." I know a guy who grew up playing tennis, and he watched with great interest as manufacturers began to make tennis rackets with larger and larger heads. The larger head made it easier to hit the ball, and therefore easier to play the game. Everybody started buying oversized rackets. The man who invented the oversized racket, whose name happens to be Howard Head, made millions with his idea.

Anyway, the guy I know watched this happen over a period of several years. During that time, he took up the game of golf, which he found most frustrating. He had no trouble hitting a moving tennis ball with an oversized racket, but he was having a terrible time trying to hit a golf ball that wasn't even moving. He finally realized that the problem was the golf club. It had a head the size of a lemon. That was several years ago. He wondered why someone hadn't developed a golf club with a larger head, like the oversized tennis rackets. He knew it was a great idea, but he didn't pursue it. Maybe he thought it was too obvious, or maybe he let someone talk him out of it. Either way, that guy was an idiot! He should have pursued his dreams. I can say that, because that guy was me!

In 1991, a man named Ely Callaway introduced the Big Bertha golf club with an oversized head. In 1993, golfers bought $250 million worth of Big Bertha golf clubs. Don't be an idiot like me. Pursue your dreams. They can come true.

Several years ago, there were 30 kids singing in the choir at the First United Methodist Church of Dallas, Texas. They all enjoyed singing on Sunday, but one 12-year-old, Laurie Gayle Stephenson, had a dream. She wanted to be a star on Broadway when she grew up. Laurie wasn't necessarily a better singer than the other 29 kids in the choir. She was just a better dreamer. Her dream became her passion and she never lost sight of it. She knew it was a long shot, but someone had convinced her that you can't make long shots if you don't take long shots. Not only that, but she did something that most people are afraid to do. She told her friends and family about her dream. That way, she didn't have to pursue her dream alone.

As with any dream, Laurie's took a lot of hard work and a great deal of dedication. As with many dreams, Laurie's came true. She eventually became the star of *Phantom of the Opera* on Broadway — the most successful play in theater history. It just goes to show you that a 12-year-old's dream is as good as anyone's.

You probably know that Michael Jordan was cut from his high school basketball team when he was 16. Now do you believe that dreams can come true?

By the way, what is *your* dream?

L ife is all about making choices. Good choices, bad choices, right choices, wrong choices. People don't always do the right thing every time they have to make a choice. That would be perfection, and nobody is perfect. There are no perfect parents, no perfect friends, no perfect teachers, no perfect brothers, and no perfect sisters. But that's okay. We're all human, and humans make mistakes every once in a while. Mistakes are part of growing up, and they're okay as long as we learn from them.

As you get older, though, the difference between right and wrong should become more clear to you. We're not talking about decisions here, like what to wear to school or what music to listen to. We're talking about choices — choices between right and wrong.

Life is loaded with choices. Will I lie to my parents? Will I cheat on my boyfriend? Will I smoke pot? Will I cheat on my math test? Life is also about facing the mirror. If you make the wrong choice and do the wrong thing, you might fool part of the crowd, or you might even fool everyone. But you'll never fool yourself, and you have to live with yourself for the rest of your life. When you look in the mirror, you can't fool you.

I used to think that there were some things that weren't totally right or totally wrong. I almost convinced myself that there were some choices that were "kind of right and sort of wrong."

I remember this one well. When I was a freshman in high school, I went to a huge party with mostly seniors. I saw nothing wrong with that. During the party, three of the seniors asked me to go for a ride with them. They were all girls, so obviously I saw nothing wrong with that either. I vaguely remember my parents telling me not to leave the party with anyone, but I guess three senior girls made my memory a little foggy. Needless to say, I got in the car. By that time, I was knee-deep in that kind of right/sort of wrong mood. When we drove off, I didn't know where we were going. But after we stopped at a fast-food restaurant, borrowed 20 rolls of toilet paper, and threw every one of them into the trees in some guy's front yard, I felt like I was waist-deep rather than knee-deep in my kind of right/sort of wrong comfort zone. Next thing I knew, there were flashing blue lights everywhere. Cops were heading our way from both ends of the street. Until that moment, blue had been my favorite color.

The first thing that came to my mind was to run. I was afraid nothing else would occur to me, so I did run — as fast and as far as I could. I left those cops so far behind that it almost seemed funny. What wasn't very funny was when I remembered that I had left my coat in the front yard. I had taken it off so I could really throw the rolls of toilet paper. Brilliant, right? Now I was sweating like crazy and it had nothing to do with my run. I was scared to death. I started to go back for my coat, but then I had an amazing thought. Why go back? For all I cared, the cops could keep the coat. Maybe one of them had a son my age. He could give my coat to him. I thought I had it all figured out. Wrong.

As I turned around to continue my midnight sprint, it suddenly occurred to me that the cop's son probably wouldn't want a coat that had a label in it with my name on it. I was busted, and I had nobody to blame but myself — although I thought about blaming it all on my mother, since she was the one who sewed the label on my coat. Walking back to the scene of the crime, I realized I had made four wrong choices: I left the party, I stole the toilet paper, I threw the toilet paper, and I ran from the cops. I also made one very bad decision. I took off my coat.

When I arrived back at the blue lights, I was thinking about my future. I could just see it on my first job application:

> **Question #6:** Have you ever been convicted of a crime? If yes, explain below.
>
> **Answer:** Yes. Petty theft (stealing toilet paper), vandalism (throwing toilet paper), littering (leaving toilet paper), trespassing, and resisting arrest.

What a future. Five crimes and a criminal record and I wasn't even 16 yet. So much for waist-deep. Now I was up to my neck in that kind of right/sort of wrong comfort zone, which wasn't so comfortable anymore.

I don't know why, but the toilet paper gods must have been with me that night. The cops called my parents and sent me home with my father at 2 A.M. I guess they thought an evening at home with my dad would be worse than an evening in jail.

The evening wasn't so bad, but the next morning was rough. My mother woke me up at 5 A.M., after only three hours of sleep. She sent me back to the scene of the crime to clean up our "little" mess, which wasn't exactly so little anymore. How was I supposed to know it was going to rain on that toilet paper all night long? The yard was a disaster. It took all day to clean up. Where are the toilet paper gods when you need them?

Luckily, I escaped the criminal record and the night in jail, but the choices I made were wrong — clearly wrong.

Wrong is wrong and right is right. And there's nothing like a few hours at the police station to help you understand the difference. Instead of trying it, you might just want to take my word on this one.

Somehow, I survived high school, graduated, and headed to the beach for my senior trip. This was obviously a time to celebrate, and a time for more choices. As I headed down the highway with two of my best friends, I had to face that kind of right/sort of wrong situation again. You would think that I would have learned by now. My friend, who was driving, was also drinking. Where I grew up, you could drink at age 18, so my friend was definitely old enough to drink, but he wasn't quite old enough to drink and drive. There's no such thing.

I'll make a long story short, because it's not a very pleasant one. At 4 A.M., traveling 60 mph, we lost control of our car, slid across the highway, and ran head on into the embankment. I don't remember closing my eyes, but I must have, because I do remember opening them. When I did, no one was talking and no one was moving. For all I knew, no one except me was living. For once in my life, I hoped I was wrong.

Somehow, all three of us survived that crash, and I really don't know why. I could have easily been killed that night. The whole ordeal only took about five seconds. It's kind of weird to think that it took me 17 years of living to get where I was, and it would have only taken five seconds to die.

As I got older, I began to see right and wrong more clearly. I finally understood that wrong choices don't become right just because you get away with them. As I cruised through my first semester in college, I made an effort to do the right thing as often as possible. Sometimes, doing the right thing means you have to go against the crowd or disagree with a friend. Real friends will respect your decision to do the right thing. If they don't, it might be time to reconsider your friendship. Peer pressure stinks. Don't let it get the best of you. You are much too strong for that. You have to be able to stand up to anyone when it comes to choosing between right and wrong.

In my first year of college, I had a friend named Benji, who was a big football star. We decided to study together for our final history exam, which I believe was worth 50 percent of our grade. Benji and I got together for two solid days before the exam. I studied all day, while Benji watched TV and talked on the phone. I couldn't believe he wasn't going to study. Maybe he thought he didn't have to study. Maybe he thought he could just sit next to me at the exam and copy my answers. Maybe he was wrong. We were friends, but I wasn't going to let him cheat. I wore a baseball cap to class the next day, and when I got my exam I put my cap on top of it. I didn't even look at Benji, who was, as expected, sitting right next to me. I covered every answer so he couldn't come close to seeing them. I finished the test before Benji did and headed out the door. I knew I had done the right thing and I also knew that Benji was going to flunk the test, but I decided that was his problem. He should have been studying instead of talking on the phone and watching TV.

I ran into Benji a few weeks later, during Christmas break. The first thing he said was, "How did you do on that history exam?" I couldn't wait for him to ask. "I made a B, just two points from an A," I bragged. Now it was my turn. "How about you?" I asked. I knew he had failed the exam, but I wanted to hear him say it. Benji shook his head and said, "I didn't do as well as I wanted to. I guess I should have studied harder. I made a high A, but I thought I had a 100."

I felt like an idiot. Turns out, Benji had already finished studying before he hooked up with me. In fact, I found out later that he was one of the smartest guys in school. He went on to become the chief financial officer for a great big company.

Oh well, at least I got a chance to practice doing the right thing.

What I have learned is that happiness is all about doing the right thing. There is no such thing as kind of right/sort of wrong. Wrong is wrong and right is right, and no amount of fun, fame, or money can change that. We all have to face the mirror some day. And you can't fool you.

count your blessings (not your money)

T eenagers have a lot to deal with these days. It seems like every time you turn around, there's another problem to face — school problems, parent problems, boyfriend and girlfriend problems, weight problems, zits, bad hair days, etc.

Unfortunately, problems are not restricted to teenagers. Everybody has problems: old people and young people, rich people and poor people, smart people and people who are not quite as smart as smart people.

Problems are a part of life, and they are not something you can avoid. They must be dealt with. Your ability to deal with them is a big part of being successful and happy. You have problems — I have problems. Everybody has problems.

As I started to write this chapter, I wasn't sure I knew all the answers about dealing with problems, so I started looking for advice. I didn't have to look far. My next-door neighbor, Patrick Lloyd, explained that we all learn to deal with problems in our own way. He told me that he learned this when he was 23. Patrick had just finished college on a baseball scholarship and had a chance to play in the major leagues. He loved to play baseball and he loved to party. He only partied occasionally, though — like seven nights a week.

It could have been any night, but it happened to be a Monday. Patrick and four of his friends headed out to party at 10 P.M. By midnight, they were all loaded. If you could smoke it, drink it, or snort it, they had done it. Just after midnight, Patrick's car came around a sharp curve. The speed limit sign on that curve read 35 mph. The speedometer in Patrick's car read 70 mph. Nobody saw the curve and nobody saw the sign. The driver was no help. What they needed was a pilot. Their car flew 50 feet as it sailed off an inclined driveway and into the air.

As you know, what goes up, must come down. Fortunately, their car landed in the middle of a great big, soft, grassy backyard. Unfortunately, there was a concrete slab right in the middle of that backyard. Two of Patrick's best friends were in the front seat. They aren't his friends anymore. They were both killed on impact. They died right there in the car.

Patrick and his two friends in the back seat survived the crash. Patrick woke up at the hospital two hours later with his mother at his side. When he woke up, he heard one of his friends screaming hysterically in the next room. He wanted to walk over and check on his friend, but it wasn't meant to be. Patrick and his two friends who survived the crash left the hospital with one thing in common — wheelchairs. All three were paralyzed and might never walk again.

The point of this story is not that Patrick and his friends went out and got loaded, or that the result of their party was two funerals and three wheelchairs. The point of the story is that my friend Patrick has been faced with a challenge that is far more difficult than any challenge most of us will probably ever face. So when Patrick was telling me how to deal with problems and bad days, I listened very carefully.

Patrick says, "In order to deal with your worst days and your biggest problems, you need to do two things. First, keep your problems in perspective and remember that no matter what your problem is, it could always be worse — much worse." Second, Patrick says, "Next time you are having a really rotten day, stop and think about someone at your school or in your community who is less fortunate than you. Think about someone who has bigger problems than you." But, more important, Patrick says, "Don't just think about them. Go out and help someone who is less fortunate than you." What my friend Patrick is talking about is young people like you volunteering your time to help others who are less fortunate than you.

> "Education is what survives when what has been learned has been forgotten."
>
> B.F. Skinner

Sometimes we don't realize how good we have it. We forget that everybody has good days and bad days. If we didn't have the bad days, maybe the good days wouldn't seem so good.

I remember one of my bad days. I was 17, my girlfriend had just broken up with me, and I thought the world was coming to an end. I couldn't imagine anything worse. I sat on my front porch and felt sorry for myself all morning. As I sat, I watched a guy and his dog jog around the block four times. On lap five, the guy stopped for his mutt to make a pit stop in my front yard. I couldn't believe it. I walked across the yard to yell at the guy, and then I saw something I'll never forget. This dog wasn't a mutt, and he wasn't making a pit stop. I was the one who felt like a mutt. The dog was just doing his job. The jogger was blind. The message was powerful.

Since that day, no problem of mine has ever overwhelmed me. Next time you think you're having a bad day, put a blindfold on and jog around the block.

Keep your problems in perspective. Remember, they could always be worse — much worse.

For many people, they are much worse. Just look around and see how many people have been dealt a hand that makes your life look like a bed of roses. If you pay close attention, you will see them everywhere. There's the homeless guy spending the winter in a cardboard box. He doesn't have a pair of NIKE high-tops; in fact, he has no shoes at all. There's the 16-year-old girl with a brain tumor. She doesn't pray for a boyfriend at night; she just prays to live another year. Then there's the guy in the hospital writing letters to his friends. He's telling them not to bother writing back because he has AIDS, and he thinks he will die before their letters arrive.

Look around and become aware of others less fortunate than you. Everyone has an obligation to act on that awareness, including teenagers. Don't feel sorry for the homeless, the AIDS patients, or those who are physically or mentally challenged. They don't need your pity. They need your acceptance and they need to feel like they are part of society. You can help them feel that way.

Your generation has already taken great steps in this area. Your concern for others is remarkable. Don't stop — don't even pause. Make community service a priority in your life. Unfortunately, some people think community service is something you do when you get to be old and rich. That's wrong. Community service is part of the journey you are all on to achieve success.

Opportunities to do for others are endless. In case you want to know what your options are, a guide to community service organizations can be found on page 91. These are all organizations that are looking for teenage volunteers. Give them a call, get involved, and tell your friends to do the same. Don't forget to volunteer at your local hospitals, feed the homeless in your city, and spend some time with the senior citizens in your area.

Helping others will help you keep your problems in perspective. The community service formula is simple: help others, learn something, meet people, and feel good.

if only I had

a second chance

At the beginning of this book, I told you that I had taken a road less traveled on my trip down the highway of trial and error. I made lots of friends. I made enough money. And yes, I made my share of mistakes. I'd like to think that I learned something from the mistakes I made. If I did, then the mistakes served a purpose. If I didn't, then my mistakes served no purpose, and I wasted time as I made each mistake. And time is something you can't buy at the store. Time is valuable. Just ask the AIDS patient who only has a few weeks to live, or the 16-year-old cancer patient who knows that this year will be her last. Time wasted is time lost.

As I wrote this book, I realized that I had lived in the fast lane, the slow lane, and almost every lane in between. Writing this book gave me a chance to look back and consider what I would do differently if I could be a teenager just one more time. Don't get me wrong. I don't really want to be a teenager again, I just want to think about it. But if I did have another shot at it, here's what I would do.

I would further my education.
It took me awhile to figure it out, but now I understand how valuable knowledge can be. While it's true that you can't simply trade a degree for success, the knowledge that you acquire in school is incredibly valuable. The business community rewards knowledge. Stay in school as long as you can.

I would become a computer wiz.
Today, communication, information, and knowledge depend greatly on computers. The computer-based information superhighway will be the road to much of your future success. This highway has no speed limit. You can go as fast as you are willing to learn. This isn't a maybe. This is for sure. Work on your computer skills and learn how to use the Internet.

I would learn a second language.
The population of the world is growing at the rate of 10,000 new people every hour. Most of them don't speak English. Success in business is starting to depend more on international relationships. It is likely that a multilingual employee will have more opportunities for success than someone who only speaks one language. Today, a second language is good to have. Tomorrow, it will be critical.

I would build a larger vocabulary.
Studies show that large vocabularies and success go hand in hand. The reason for this is simple. A large vocabulary is not just about big words. It's about lots of words — big and little — and knowing how and when to use them. A large vocabulary enables you to communicate on all levels. How successful you become will depend on your ability to communicate with the president of a company as well as the stock clerk in the warehouse. Learn two new words each week. That's 104 new words each year. Do this until you hit the real world and you will be way ahead of the game.

I would have more balance in my life.
I would balance my time between work, play, family, and friends — and not necessarily in that order. Good health depends on a balanced life. The average person doesn't figure this out until it's way too late. Don't be average.

I would read more.
Reading serves several purposes. It builds your vocabulary, makes you more interesting, and guarantees that you will never be bored. Read everything you possibly can.

I would learn to sell.
Most people don't think they will be in sales when they grow up. Most people are wrong. Almost everybody sells something in their job. They either sell a product or a service. Professional athletes sell a service. Record stores sell a product. Doctors sell a service. Artists sell a product. But more than anything, we all have to sell ourselves. Selling is selling. If you learn to sell something, you can probably sell anything. It's like riding a bike: once you learn, you never forget.

I would work on my public-speaking skills.
Most of us don't intend to be public speakers, but every time you open your mouth to talk you are publicly speaking. The only exceptions are talking to yourself and talking in your sleep. Both of these are a little weird, but maybe these are good ways to privately practice your public speaking. Whether you're talking to a group of 100 or just talking to one person, your speaking skills will be critical. The first time you talk to anyone, you will make a first impression, and first impressions are never forgotten.

There you have it. That's what I would do if I had a second chance. Remember, the more prepared you are for your first chances, the less need you will have for second chances.

the bottom line

The real world will be here before you know it. Hopefully, you now understand what success is and what it takes to succeed. The real world is not as tough as it sounds. In fact, it's pretty cool, if you come prepared.

So what's the bottom line? Actually, there are 12 bottom lines To make a long story short, give these a try:

1. Find your passion.
2. Buy an address book and fill it.
3. Meet all kinds of people.
4. Ask a million questions.
5. Stay in touch with everyone.
6. Read everything you can.
7. Uncover your natural talents.
8. Try a few jobs before college or university.
9. Dream and pursue your dreams.
10. Always do the right thing.
11. Volunteer for community service.
12. Remember, success is a journey, not a destination.

looking ahead

To teenagers everywhere:

You were born into a world that's kind of screwed up. I don't know if it's a result of ignorance, greed, or selfishness. I suspect it's a little of each. Your generation is faced with a staggering divorce rate, frightening school violence, an environmental mess, and a health care crisis, just to name a few. You didn't ask for any of these problems, and no one bothered to ask if you wanted them. Unfortunately, they were here when you arrived.

This probably doesn't seem fair, but as I'm sure you know, life isn't always fair. And it's not always easy, either. There are always new challenges to deal with and obstacles to overcome.

My gut feeling is that your generation will deal with the challenges and overcome the obstacles, because yours is not a generation of ignorance, greed, or selfishness. I believe your generation will start fixing the world, and the next generation will thank you.

Good luck to each of you.

Extra Stuff

HABITAT FOR HUMANITY INTERNATIONAL
121 Habitat Street
Americus, GA 31709
(912) 924-6935
www.habitat.org

What They Do:
Habitat for Humanity was started in 1976. Former President Jimmy Carter is their most famous volunteer. This organization builds houses for poor people who can't afford their own homes. This helps them move out of high-crime areas and into clean, safe neighborhoods. Habitat for Humanity is one of the most highly respected community service organizations in North America.

What You Can Do:
Even if you don't know which end of the hammer to hold, you can help build houses with other volunteers. It's a great way to learn how a home is built so when you do hit it big in the real world, you can build your own dream home. (Hint: It might also be a great place to make some valuable contacts.)

Between building projects, you can distribute information about Habitat for Humanity to classmates, church groups, and friends. If you have a group that wants to help, call the Habitat for Humanity office and they will send someone out to talk to you.

How to Find Them:
Habitat for Humanity has offices in all 50 states. Check the business pages of your phone book for their number. If you have no luck there, call the main office at (912) 924-6935.

MAKE-A-WISH FOUNDATION
100 West Clarendon
Suite 2200, Phoenix AZ 85013
(800) 722-9474
www.wish.org

What They Do:
Terminally ill children are kids who have an illness that can't be cured. They will die soon. Since these kids can't wish themselves well, Make-A-Wish Foundation lets them make a wish for something else — like a trip to Disney World or lunch with Michael Jordan. Make-A-Wish Foundation puts together a "wish team" to make the wish come true.

What You Can Do:
Make-A-Wish Foundation has over 11,000 volunteers nationwide and would like to add you to their team. You can be on a "wish team," help recruit other team members, or work on special fund-raising events. Maybe you know someone who deserves a wish. If you only had one year to live, wouldn't you want someone like you on your "wish team"?

How to Find Them:
There are 79 Make-A-Wish Foundation chapters in the United States. Call (800) 722–9474 and ask for the volunteer coordinator.

AMERICAN RED CROSS
National Headquarters
430 17th St. NW Street
Washington, D.C. 20006
(202) 737–8300
www.redcross.org

What They Do:

What do forest fires, floods, earthquakes, tornadoes, hurricanes, and plane crashes all have in common? They all send the Red Cross into action. Victims of these disasters are helped by the Red Cross and its volunteers.

What You Can Do:

You can join the Disaster Youth Corps. This group helps prepare communities for natural disasters. You can fill sandbags, help with fund-raisers, learn CPR and first aid, and then teach your friends. You can also get involved in peer-to-peer education about AIDS-related topics that pertain to teenagers. If a tornado hits your house tomorrow, you will appreciate the Red Cross. Maybe it would be a good idea to show your appreciation before you need them.

How to Find Them:

There are 2,400 chapters across the country. Check your local business pages for the chapter nearest you. Ask to speak to the volunteer coordinator.

MUSCULAR DYSTROPHY ASSOCIATION
3300 East Sunrise Drive
Tucson, AZ 89718
(800) 572-1717
www.mdausa.org

What They Do:

The Muscular Dystrophy Association is a partnership between scientists and concerned citizens. Their goal is to find cures for diseases that affect the muscles. Some people with muscular dystrophy can't walk, talk, or even brush their own teeth. The Muscular Dystrophy Association has a huge fund-raiser every Labor Day. It's a 24-hour telethon on national TV hosted by Jerry Lewis.

What You Can Do:

The Muscular Dystrophy Association has summer camps all over the country. Each camper with muscular dystrophy hangs out with a volunteer camper and they enjoy camp activities together. There are fund-raisers for the Muscular Dystrophy Association throughout the year like Walk-A-Thons, Bowl-A-Thons, etc. If you're not sure that you want to volunteer, think about the kids with muscular dystrophy who can't even walk. Maybe that will help you make up your mind.

How to Find Them:
Check the local business pages for the chapter in your area. If you have any trouble, call (800) 572–1717.

THE AIDS MEMORIAL QUILT AND AIDS EDUCATION
(The Names Project Foundation)
P.O. Box 14573
San Francisco, CA 94114
(415) 882–5500
www.luna-imaging.com/names

What They Do:
The Quilt, as it is now called, is a memorial to those who have died of AIDS. The Quilt is made up of thousands of panels that are put together like pieces of a puzzle. Each panel includes information about a person who has died of AIDS. I saw the Quilt exhibit in Washington, D.C. It was bigger than ten football fields, side by side. The Quilt is displayed at schools, malls, etc., all over America. The purpose of the Quilt is to educate the public about AIDS and AIDS prevention.

What You Can Do:
The Quilt requires hundreds of volunteers to assemble and disassemble when it is on display in each city. You can help with this process or you can hand out information to people who come to see the Quilt. Or, if you knew someone who died from AIDS, you can make a Quilt panel in his or her honor.

How to Find Them:
Call (415) 882–5500 and ask for the volunteer coordinator. If you want to volunteer for other local AIDS organizations, call the National Aids Hotline at (800) 342–2437.

STUDENTS AGAINST DRUNK DRIVING
P.O. Box 8702
Clinton, IA 52736
(508) 481–3568

What They Do:
More teenagers die in car crashes than from anything else. Half of all fatal crashes are drug or alcohol related. Every 24 minutes, someone in America is killed by a drunk driver. Students Against Drunk Driving is a great organization with seven million members.

What You Can Do:
The 25,000 SADD chapters are run by students. It's all about believing that, yes, it can happen to you. As a SADD member, your job is to convince other students not to drink and drive and not to ride with anyone who has been drinking. And obviously, all SADD members make their own commitment not to drink and drive and to never ride with someone who is drinking. Every teenager should be a member — even you. Don't wait until one of your friends is a victim of a drunk driver to get involved.

How to Find Them:
Call Students Against Drunk Driving at (508) 481–3568 for information about chapters in your area. If there is not one, ask SADD to send a guest speaker to your school to talk about starting a chapter.

SPECIAL OLYMPICS INTERNATIONAL
1325 G Street
Suite 500
Washington, DC 20005
(800) 700–2258
www.specialolympics.org

What They Do:
Special Olympics provides athletic training and competition for children and adults with mental retardation. The program helps these people get in shape, build self-esteem, develop skills, and make friends. For many people with mental retardation, Special Olympics is the happiest part of their lives. Today, almost one million Special Olympics athletes take part in 23 Olympic-type sports year-round.

What You Can Do:

There are 500,000 Special Olympics volunteers worldwide. More are needed. If you know a lot about sports, you would be a great Special Olympics volunteer. If you know nothing about sports, you would still be a great Special Olympics volunteer. There's something to do for everyone. You can help coach the Special Olympics athletes. You can be a cheerleader at the Special Olympics games in your city or state. All Special Olympics athletes who compete get a hug whether they win, lose, or tie. That's why these games are "special."

How to Find Them:

Special Olympics was established by President John F. Kennedy's sister, Eunice Kennedy Shriver. She started this great organization in 1968 near Washington, D.C., so that's where Special Olympics' headquarters is located. Every state has a chapter, so call (800) 700–2258 for information on your state chapter.

THE HUMANE SOCIETY
(American Society for the Prevention of Cruelty to Animals—ASPCA)
441 East 92nd Street
New York, NY 10128
(212) 876–7700
www.aspca.org

What They Do:

The Humane Society takes care of lost, stray, or unwanted animals. This is where you go to adopt a pet.

What You Can Do:

Nobody wants to adopt a pet that doesn't like people, so volunteers at the Humane Society keep animals "people-friendly" by playing with them, feeding them, walking them, etc. The Humane Society also holds fund-raisers like the "Pet Parade," which uses lots of volunteers.

How to Find Them:

Your local Humane Society is usually listed in the business pages under your city's name. For example, if you live in Boston, look under the "B's" for the Boston Humane Society. If that doesn't work, call the ASPCA at (212) 876–7700 for help.

UNITED CEREBRAL PALSY ASSOCIATIONS

1660 L Street, NW
Suite 700
Washington, DC 20036
(800) 872–5827
www.ucpa.org

What They Do:

Cerebral palsy can result from an injury to the brain or from a lack of oxygen to an unborn child during pregnancy or delivery. People with cerebral palsy may have trouble walking or controlling the movements in their arms and legs. They might also have a tough time hearing or seeing. United Cerebral Palsy provides family support, education, and training for people with cerebral palsy.

What You Can Do:

Kids with cerebral palsy want to feel accepted and want to feel like they are part of the community. They are just like you and me. They need friends to talk to and hang out with. You can go to the mall together or head out to a movie. Kids with cerebral palsy can do lots of things that other kids do, sometimes even more. My friend, Chris Williams, is ten years old and lives in North Carolina. He has cerebral palsy, but last summer he paddled a canoe seven miles down a river. You can easily get involved with some of the great cerebral palsy fund-raisers like the Bike-A-Thons and Basketball Shoot-A-Thons.

How to Find Them:

There are 255 Cerebral Palsy chapters across the country. Call (800) 872–5827 for information on the chapter nearest you.

BEST BUDDIES

100 S.E. 2nd Street
Suite 1990
Miami, FL 33131
(800) 892–8339
www.bestbuddies.org

What They Do:

There are 7.5 million people in the United States with mental retardation. It's not their fault. They were born that way. One of the most exciting things a person with mental retardation can do is make a friend from outside the circle of mental retardation. This is where Best Buddies comes in. They introduce college students to people with mental retardation. The college student then becomes friends with the person with mental retardation.

What You Can Do:

If you're at least a college freshman, you can get a "buddy." It's easy. Just take your "buddy" along as you do whatever you normally do — go to the mall, the movies, a concert, etc. It's the feeling of acceptance that makes your "buddy" feel good. Most volunteers see their "buddies" twice a month. If you're not in college yet, you can volunteer at the Best Buddies chapter in your area.

How to Find Them:

There are 170 Best Buddies chapters on college campuses across the United States. Call Best Buddies Headquarters at (800) 892–8339 for information on the chapter in your area.

These are all great organizations. I have worked with several of them. There are many others that you might want to consider. To do so, call your local United Way office or the United Way headquarters at (800) 895–2822. They will fill you in on all the community service organizations in your area, based on what your particular interests are.

one last thank you

Nobody accomplishes anything without support. This book is no exception. The project would never have started, would not have continued, and certainly would not have been finished without the help of many special people.

My sincere thanks to everyone at The Galloway School in Atlanta, Georgia, for their support at every stage of the game; to David Brantley, who didn't exactly pull me out of the gutter but who did expose me to many of the ideas conveyed in this book; to Robynn Greer, for her vision and unconditional support; to John Day, my friend and teenage sounding board; to Monica James, for her help and encouragement; and most important, to God, for all of the great experiences He has blessed me with.

PARENTS
and
EDUCATORS

Chad Foster's nationally acclaimed speaking presentation is now available on videotape for use in the classroom or at home. This 27-minute motivational video has inspired more than 500,000 teenagers to pursue their dreams, learn to communicate, explore careers, make good choices, and volunteer for community service. Chad is the ultimate storyteller and delivers his powerful messages with sincere passion and kid-cool humor. To order the *"Chad Foster Live"* video, please use the order form found on the next page or visit our website at www.chad-foster.com.

Chad Foster speaks to more than 100,000 students and educators each year. To schedule Chad for a live speaking engagement, please contact us at (770) 761-8794 or through our website at **www.chadfoster.com**.

teenagers – preparing for the real world

ORDER FORM

TO ORDER,
Call (770) 761-8794
Fax (770) 761-9865

Fax or send your purchase order to:

Teenagers — Preparing for the Real World
P.O. Box 1408
Conyers, GA 30012

STUDENT BOOK	
ISBN: 0-9644456-0-3	
1-10 copies	$11.00 per copy *
10-99 copies	$8.50 per copy *
100+ copies	$7.00 per copy *
TEACHER'S GUIDE	
$30.00 per copy *	
PRESENTATION VIDEO	
$60.00 per copy *	

* Prices subject to change without notice.

To order the Spanish version of
Teenagers—Preparing for the Real World
call (770) 761-8794

■ **SHIP TO:**

NAME

JOB TITLE

SCHOOL NAME

STREET ADDRESS

CITY   STATE   ZIP

( )
TELEPHONE

E-MAIL

■ **BILL TO** *(if different from SHIP TO)*:

NAME

SCHOOL NAME

STREET ADDRESS

CITY   STATE   ZIP

( )
TELEPHONE

E-MAIL

■ **PAYMENT OPTIONS:**

❑ PURCHASE ORDER ATTACHED: #_____

❑ CHECK ENCLOSED
   (Make check payable to Teenagers Preparing for the Real World)

ISBN	PRODUCT	QUANTITY	UNIT PRICE	TOTAL
			$	$
			$	$
			$	$
			$	$
			Total Cost of Items:	$
			Shipping/Handling (Add 10%): (Minimum Shipping $4.00)	$
			TOTAL:	$

VISIT US ONLINE
@
www.chadfoster.com